Lipstick Ghetto

Lipstick Ghetto

THE GIRLS' GUIDE TO ESCAPING the '9 to 5' Rat Race

STACEY SMITH

iUniverse, Inc.
New York Bloomington Shanghai

Lipstick Ghetto
The Girls' Guide To Escaping the '9 to 5' Rat Race

iUniverse books may be ordered through booksellers or by contacting:

iUniverse
1663 Liberty Drive
Bloomington, IN 47403
www.iuniverse.com
1-800-Authors (1-800-288-4677)

Because of the dynamic nature of the Internet, any Web addresses or links contained in this book may have changed since publication and may no longer be valid.

The views expressed in this work are solely those of the author and do not necessarily reflect the views of the publisher, and the publisher hereby disclaims any responsibility for them.

ISBN: 978-0-595-50772-6 (pbk)
ISBN: 978-0-595-61643-5 (ebk)

Printed in the United States of America

Acknowledgements

First of all I want to thank God for His abundant Mercy and Grace. I also want to thank my mother, Sandra Smith, for giving birth to me. I wouldn't be here without you!

I'd like to thank my late-great grandmother, Mary Smith, who cared for and loved me as her daughter. You are an eternal example of a life well-lived. I will forever be indebted to you for the sacrifices you made for me. I miss you and love you!

I also want to thank my late-aunt, Wendy Caldwell, who taught me the importance of learning and achievement. I'll never forget your support during good times and bad. Thank you for the sacrifices you made for me and my brothers and sister. I love you, always!

I'd also like to thank the three best bosses I had during my time in the Lipstick Ghetto™. Pam Stanley, who recognized my potential and gave me a chance to increase my earning potential beyond what I had ever earned. I'd also like to thank other bosses (James Lemons and Mark Roter) who accepted me for me … even though I didn't quite fit into the "corporate mold."

Why I wrote this book

Throughout my working life I've spoken to many women who've stated that they would love to be doing something else with their time than working in the "Rat Race." Some of the reasons they've given for not pursing their passions include: not marrying a rich enough man, or that their husband doesn't work at all, or because they're too old.

Some of these women, though they wouldn't admit it—were just down-right afraid to step out of their comfort zones and live out their God-given destiny.

This book is intended to motivate, inspire and be a "kick in the pants" to women around the world to stop making excuses and to start creating a life that works.

If you're one of the millions of women who are stuck between a dream and a job … this book will provide a holistic approach to moving beyond fear and your self-limiting beliefs. The book also provides a step-by-step approach to turning your passion into profit. My goal is to help every woman attain health, wealth, and knowledge of self. (3 John, verse 2)

You Can Do It

Whether you want to get rich or just earn extra money each month—there are many ways and opportunities to turn your passions and interests into cash. With a computer, a little time, and an internet connection, you can open just about any type of business you want with very little money.

From opening your own web store (stores.ebay.com, dropshipdesign.com or amazonservices.com) to publishing books and eBooks (iuniverse.com, booksurge. com, snapfish.com, payloadz.com), to selling t-shirts (cafepress.com, zazzle.com, spreadshirt.com and threadless.com) to starting a membership site (membership-siteadvisor.com and SentryLogin.com) … the "eWorld" is your oyster!

According to the Center for Women's Business Research, in 2007, women owned a 51% share in over 7 million companies—with sales topping $1.1 trillion. So as you begin your journey to entrepreneurship … know you're in good company. This is especially true for my African-American sisters. According to former U.S. Labor Secretary, Alexis Herman (also a sister), the number of businesses owned by black women has increased 147% between 1997 and 2006—compared to the 24% overall growth rate for other groups! You can do it too.

All the Best & God Bless,

Stacey Smith

Introduction

What is the Lipstick Ghetto™? The Lipstick Ghetto™ is any career path that limits a woman's ability to live her best life. The Lipstick Ghetto is a place of confinement and limitation. Women working in the **Lipstick Ghetto™ often feel like they're stuck between a dream and a job.** Escaping the Lipstick Ghetto™ produces an **abundance of time and money** for more important pursuits (i.e. raising children, travel, philanthropic involvement, etc.)

Whether you're a woman who doesn't have the **time** to spend your six-figure salary or a woman who doesn't have **money** to send your children to college—you have some difficult choices to make and new risks to take.

This book is set up as a 4-week, holistic program, where you'll learn how to get over your doubts, fears and take POSITVE ACTION towards realizing your dreams. This book will give you the courage you need to step out of your comfort zone. It will also give you practical tips on turning your passion into a tangible and viable business You'll also learn **how to use the relationships, opportunities and gifts already in your life to achieve your goals.**

Take this book with you throughout your work week. It's compact enough to put in your purse so that you can read it on the go (i.e. during your lunch break, waiting in line at the grocery store or under the dryer at the salon).

Also, consider getting a gift copy for a girlfriend who's been thinking about changing her life. Then meet to discuss each others' progress.

Contents

5-Step Quick Start Guide

Use these 5 steps to help kick-start your creative juices and as a foundation for the rest of the book. Also for other resources, check out this book's companion site at www.LipstickGhetto.com.

1. Change Your Mind. When you change your mind about your life, you will change your life—for good. Don't let one job, goal, relationship, or circumstance be the end-all, be-all to your existence. What you're doing right now is just a stepping stone to what's up next. I want you to start thinking outside the box while you're still working in one.

Feeling stuck is a signal that you need to do something different. It can be easy to feel trapped by your current situation, but with creativity and commitment you can get OUT of any rut you've gotten into.

2. Live by 'Less Is More.' The popular catch-phrase "Time Management" has created a class of women who are constantly busy, yet unfulfilled and frustrated. Why? Fitting more activity into your day doesn't necessarily translate into progress.

The best life is usually built by subtraction—not addition. Determine what's important and get rid of the rest. Too much of anything (activity, possessions, etc.) zaps your energy. Thus, keeping you from bringing your best self to what you really want to do.

3. Underestimate obstacles/Emphasize your strengths. In order to underestimate the obstacles to becoming financially free—you need to know what they are. Get a piece of paper and write a list of the top three hurdles to your success. Then write a possible solution to overcoming each hurdle. Set this paper aside.

Now, for the next 4 weeks, I want you to only focus on leveraging your strengths (i.e. what you're good at/what you DO have).... rather than trying to fix or overcome your obstacles. Fixating on obstacles will ultimately lead to you making up excuses to do nothing.

4. Keep a Dream Journal. Writing down what you want will be a tremendous help in fleshing out your plans. Use your journal to jot down all of your desires, ideas, plans, etc. You probably want to stuff your journal with newspaper and magazine articles that catch your eye (for whatever reason—don't censor your muse).

Overtime, you'll revisit, revise, and refine your Dream Journal ... but start one today! You'll be surprised by the increased motivation it brings, as well as serendipitous events (Happy Accidents) that cross your path!

5. Refuse to Settle. Giving up is not an option. If you feel overwhelmed by the process of creating the life you want, it may be because you're trying to do too much at one time. Pause, step back, and break action-items down into smaller more manageable steps. There will be distractions, delays, and setbacks, but don't let them stop you from escaping the Lipstick Ghetto™.

STEP #1

RECONNECT:
GET TO KNOW THE REAL YOU

What's Covered:

- Uncover Your Bind Spots
- The Number One Obstacle to Your Success
- Dealing with Your Insecurities & Feelings of Inadequacy

Uncovering Your Blind Spots

How do you get to know someone? You ask them questions, of course. Whether you're an online dater or interviewing a job candidate—the right questions are key tools for discovery. Getting to know yourself is no different.

**Be warned. This is one of the most 'question-intensive' sections of the book. You may want to answer them over the course of a couple of days. But, if you're an over-achiever like me, you'll probably want to answer them all now. It's up to you.

Your blind spots are the **unbecoming, self-defeating self-sabotaging, and unproductive** thoughts and behaviors that keep you from living your best life. For the most part, blind spots are subconsciously created by our unmet needs for love, attention, influence, power, or control.

Blind spots usually have to do with "fear/safety" issues. We tend to compensate for our blind spots by taking the "easy road" in life (and love) so we don't have to get out of our comfort zone. Even if this road doesn't bring fulfillment, it's easier than stepping out and stretching toward a better life.

Below are some questions to help you identify your blind spots. Real change can only occur when you are honest with yourself, so don't feel the need to censor your responses. I believe that the fastest and easiest way to change the answers you get—is to change the questions you ask.…

Ask yourself these questions:

1. How are my **attitudes and assumptions** limiting my life's progress?

   _____

   _____

2. What problems/situations am I **tolerating**? Why am I tolerating them?

   _____

   _____

3. What problems/situations am I **avoiding**? Why am I avoiding them?

   _____

   _____

4. What recurring problems/situations am I **ignoring**? Why am I ignoring them?

   _____

   _____

5. What can I do to be more proactive in **addressing the problems** in my life??

   _____

   _____

6. **Do I like** the woman I am becoming? Why or Why not?

   _____

   _____

7. What lies (from Satan, other people, society, etc.) do you believe about yourself?

   _____

   _____

8. What do I **refuse** to see about myself?

   _____

   _____

9. If others were **honest with me**, what would they tell me about myself?

   _____

   _____

10. How am I being **dishonest with myself** with regard to my career, life, health, relationships, etc.?

    _____

    _____

11. What am I **hiding** from? What am I hiding behind?

_____

_____

12. Do I go into situations **expecting** a negative outcome? If so, why?

_____

_____

13. Do I **cheat myself** out of experiencing wonderful relationships because I'm constantly worrying about others' opinion of me? If so, why?

_____

_____

14. How has being "**realistic**" kept me from living the life I want?

_____

_____

15. What **one thing** can I do **today** to improve my life?

_____

_____

16. Where will I be **in 5 years**, if I continue on my current path?

_____

_____

17. What price am I **paying for neglecting** my wants/desires?

_____

_____

The #1 Obstacle to Your Success

I believe that the number one obstacle that hinders women's success is fear. Fear will keep you in low-paying and unfulfilling work that ultimately drains you of any desire to improve your situation.

What is fear? Webster's defines it as: Alarm caused by expectation of danger. A state of dread or awe.

Another definition of F.E.A.R that I've heard Pastor Paula White use is: False Evidence Appearing Real

Top 7 Fears That Paralyze Dreams

1. Fear of failure (Feel the fear and do it anyway)
2. Fear of not being smart enough (**see next section on feelings of inadequacy)
3. Fear of not being able to perform (**see next section on feelings of inadequacy)
4. Fear of change (Read/Listen to book, "Who Moved My Cheese?")
5. Fear of Being too old (It's never to late to be what you might have been)
6. Fear of being too young (Often it's the youth who bring about change)
7. Fear of not having enough time/money/experience etc. (Make time to make money!) FYI: As I write this, I'm an Admin Assistant with workdays that begin at 3 a.m. and end a 6 p.m., so again—you <u>must make time</u> to make more money!

The Results of Fear

-   Procrastination
-   Lowered self-confidence
-   Feeling confused
-   Feeling anxious
-   Feeling insecure and inadequate
-   Negative thinking and speaking

Steps to Overcoming Your Fears

1. Determine what your fears are
2. Develop an action plan that breaks goals down into small steps
3. Take action everyday towards being your very best

<u>Words to Live By</u>:

"Courage is fear that has said it's prayers."
—**Dorothy Bernard**

"Be fearless. Your life is only limited by what you believe is possible. Outsmart your limitations by re-focusing your attention to your strengths and God's power working in you. As Nike says, 'Just Do It!' And I'll add—**'Do it NOW!'**"
—**Stacey Smith**

God has not given us a Spirit of fear, but of Power, Love & a Sound Mind …
—**2 Timothy 1:7**

Dealing with Your Insecurities & Feelings of Inadequacy

We all have things that we don't do as well as someone else. God created us with different gifts and talents so that we can help each other. I compare it to the human body. Each body part has a different function. We have eyes to see, ears to hear, a mouth to speak, feet to walk, etc.

Not everyone can be a mouth. If we all were the "mouthpiece," there wouldn't be anything for the feet or hands to do. All of our talents are needed. We need visionaries, speakers, encouragers, helpers, builders, comforters, teachers, etc.

Nonetheless, feelings of inadequacy are very real. Whether you're an administrative assistant, waitress or nurse—there are things that other people can do better than you.

I've never been a "numbers" person, but I l really enjoy watching CNBC (a business and financial news channel). I don't own a television and this is probably my most missed station. In fact, my Match.com screen name was 'CNBCWoman'! (FYI: My favorite hosts are Maria Bartiromo, Donny Deutsch, and Suze Orman, and Jim Cramer).

My point? Although I feel inadequate about my abilities to be a stockbroker or accountant—I don't let that stop me from having an interest in the world of wealth creation. Nor did I let these feelings stop me from writing this book!

Recognizing your limitations will only help you down the line … because you won't waste time trying to fix them, but you'll focus on what you can do; and let God do the rest.

Sometimes feelings of inadequacy lurk behind perfectionism. Ask yourself these questions to uncover and overcome your feelings of doubt.

- How often do you worry about your ability to accomplish your dreams?

  _____

- Do you accept your imperfections? If not, why?

  _____

- How do you handle failure, setbacks and delays in life? (blame others, blame blame yourself, try harder, blame circumstances, accept & move on etc.)

  _____

- Do you consider yourself a perfectionist? If so, has it been helpful to you? If it hasn't been helpful, why not?

  _____

Feelings of inadequacy can lead to low self esteem and decreased energy. The key is remembering that the most important relationship you will ever have (next to your relationship with God)—is the relationship that you have with yourself. You can be your closest friend or worst enemy. It's up to you.

Low self-esteem hinders your ability to achieve success. Red flags of low self-esteem include: Fear of rejection/abandonment, un-necessary self-protection, inability to recognize personal wants and needs, settling for less than you really want, development of self-destructive thinking/behavior patterns, etc.

Keys to Self-Acceptance

Failure is only temporary. The most successful people in life are those who have failed countless times—before getting it right. I had several business and personal failures (including being homeless), before succeeding with this book!

Here are some keys to 'letting go' and moving on:

- Accept that you will make mistakes
- Accept that you are not and won't ever be perfect

- Accept what you cannot change
- Accept that not everyone will agree with or support your dream
- Accept that success is a life-long journey and not a destination
- Accept that your ability to be adaptable and teachable will go a long way

<u>**Words to Live By**</u>:

"We secretly generate the results we think we deserve.
We change the results, when we change our beliefs."
—Dr. Phil

God doesn't call the qualified—He *qualifies* the called.
—Unknown

"Remember that fear always lurks behind perfectionism. Confronting
your fears and allowing yourself to be human, can paradoxically make you
a far happier and productive person"
—Dr. David M. Burn

"To live a creative life, we must lose our fear of being wrong."
—Joseph Chilton Pearce

"Often our low status in life is not because our abilities are inferior,
but because our opinion of ourselves is inferior."
—Norman Vincent Peale

"Take what I've been through … to see that you can't hold a good woman down"
—Mary J. Blige (From Breakthrough CD)

<u>Bottom Line</u>: Don't focus on your inadequacies. (What you focus on is magnified.) Focus on your strengths and how to turn your passion into dollars!

STEP #2

TAKE CARE OF YOU

What's Covered:

- Mind: What To Do When You're Lonely, Bored, or Stressed
- Body: The No More Excuses! Health Program
- Spirit: Your Divine Guide: The Holy Spirit/Intuition

Taking Care of YOU

Escaping the **Lipstick Ghetto**™ is an "inside job". Meaning that you must take care of your whole self (Mind, Body and Spirit). I know there that there will be some women who read this section and think that it has absolutely nothing to do with starting a business. However, I believe that you must look inward to move upward.

Starting a business can be a very stressful. In the beginning of your entrepreneurial journey, you're going to be doing a great deal of work on your own and it's going to be tempting to neglect your wellness needs. You must learn how to practice self care both as you start your business and after it's up and running. It all has to do with balance and pacing yourself.

YOUR MIND

On your path towards wealth and financial freedom, you're going to encounter emotional ups and downs. You have **TWO CHOICES**: You can choose the emotional discomfort of where you are or you can choose the emotional discomfort of stretching yourself beyond your comfort zone and current circumstances.

What to do when you're lonely, bored or stressed ...

<u>LONELY?</u>: Despite our interactive world of social networking, loneliness is an epidemic in this country. Being lonely has nothing to do with the number of friends you have on MySpace or connections in your LinkedIn profile. Feelings of loneliness arise out of our natural need for meaningful connections with God and others.

** Warning: As you begin your journey to escape the **Lipstick Ghetto**™, there are going to times when you feel isolated and alone because:

- The first phases of starting a business can be very solitary times.
- Not everyone will agree with or support you.

Two Ways to Beat Loneliness:

1. Reconnect with God. Taking time to connect with God on a daily basis is essential for combating feelings of being alone.

2. Reconnect with others. Develop/maintain relationships with trusted people who have your best interest at heart. Have regular dinners with family and/or close friends. Go thrift store shopping with some girlfriends (Online shopping has managed to diminish this ancient female-boding ritual). Visit the elderly in nursing homes (you'll have a chance to brighten their day!) Develop a networking group in your neighborhood.

<u>BORED?</u>: Boredom can be a dangerous condition. Some studies have linked it to conditions from drug abuse, eating disorders, pre-mature aging, depression, and even to heart attack. As you begin to plan your escape from the Lipstick Ghetto™, you are going to grow increasingly more bored with your job. The excitement and allure of starting your own business can eclipse the "drudgery" of your '9-to-5' gig.

Your boredom may be manifested as fatigue, body aches & pains, and feelings of sadness or apathy. Because boredom is a silent condition, you may sense that something's wrong in your life—but not be able to put a finger on it. So how do you get over your "the blahs" and get a new lease on life? I'm glad you asked. Here you go …

7 Ways to Get out of Your Rut:

1. **Jump-start your day.** Begin your day by doing moving meditations such as yoga or pilates. Spice up your Commute: If you take public transit to work, read a book that improves your life in some way. If you drive, listen to an audio book.

2. **Use your breaks.** Lunch breaks are a great times to practice self-care. Go on a 'prayer walk,' where you spend time talking and listening to God. Read success stories of people you admire.

3. **Add variety to your job.** Ask you boss if there are opportunities for you to get 'cross-trained' on tasks outside of your normal job duties. The newness of the work will bring new mental stimulation and challenge. You may even position yourself for a raise or promotion—which means you can

make and save more money, which will speed up your ability to leave the **Lipstick Ghetto**™.

4. **Take a day off.** Sometimes taking a 'mental health' day will help you get excited about your life and future. Use your mental health day as time to re-discover forgotten hobbies and interests. But don't do this too often, too much idle time can be counter-productive to your goals if you aren't using it wisely. Wasting time is not going to help you create a life that works

5. **Turn off the TV.** Television watching can be fun and educational. But too much time in front of the tube is mind numbing and promotes feelings of boredom. Flipping channels on a perfectly good Saturday/Sunday morning is not the way toward escaping the **Lipstick Ghetto**™. Spend your down-time on reading, studying, planning and acting on creating a better present and future.

6. **Reach out.** Volunteer for a marathon or at your favorite non-profit. Stuffing envelopes or answering their phones is an excellent way to meet new people and develop new interests. Be genuinely interested in what other people are doing. Try to help when you can, be sure not to overextend yourself.

7. **Make it fun!** Find ways to liven up your daily/weekly chores, such as laundry, meetings, exercising, house/yard work, etc. Put on your iPod and dance the 'yawn' out of mowing the lawn!

<u>STRESSED?</u>: We've talked about dealing with loneliness and boredom, now I'll discuss how you can more effectively deal with stress. Believe me, starting a business can be a stressful process. Stress is a common problem in today's 24/7 world, even for women who are not entrepreneurs. Trying to do too much, worrying about finances, etc. all can contribute to feelings of stress and anxiety.

How do you know that you are stressed/anxious? Feelings of anxiety can cause constant worry, muscle tension, trouble falling asleep, headaches, muscle twitching/trembling, intense/irrational fears, irritability, fatigue, and difficulty concentrating.

So what can you do about it? Change your approach to life's up's and downs. Being fixated on what's wrong (i.e. what you don't have etc.) only compounds your stress level.

By understanding how your thinking patterns contribute to your feelings of anxiety and learning to react differently to your stress triggers—you can make great progress towards achieving your dreams.

Think about how do you normally respond when things don't seem to be working out or seem to take a turn for the worse?

___Panic/Worry

___Ignore/Deny the situation

___Pray for guidance/Meditate

___Get angry or bitter

___Get gloomy or depressed

___Overeat

___Abuse drugs or alcohol

___Write in a Journal

___Call a friend/family member

___Work/Strive harder to turn things around

___Other _____

It's very important to deal with stress/anxiety as quickly as possible—because if left to "fester", it will affect more than your mood. It will affect your thinking, actions, and body.

Oftentimes, stress/anxiety is wrapped up in unresolved fear. Learning to address the issues beneath your stress/anxiety will go a long way in managing it. For me, stressing about how to make my business succeed consumed a lot of my energy. So much so, I wasn't concentrating on developing workable solutions.

8 Keys to Dealing with Stress and Anxiety

1. **Major on the majors**. Determine what your priorities are and focus on them. Attempting to be all things to all people will wear you out. Learning to say 'no' is a skill that every woman must learn. Don't say 'yes' when you really should say 'no.' (More on this later)

2. **Make decisions**. Don't procrastinate in your decision making. Leaving decisions 'hanging in the air' will weigh you down. This doesn't mean you

don't have to think things through or gather facts—it does mean that as soon as you are able, you make a decision. This includes responding to awaiting emails/voicemail messages!

3. **Do your own thing.** Don't let other people dictate your priorities and how you spend your time. Of course you need to be responsible to your immediate household, but trying to juggle too many balls will ultimately result in you dropping them all.

4. **Practice self-care.** I know this keeps coming up. But so many women fail to do it. But if you don't care for you, no one else will. Take responsibility for your own wellness and joy. Remember you are where you are because of your own thoughts, choices and conduct. Choose to live life well.

5. **Practice Generosity & Gratitude**. When you're open and generous to others, you're sure to make meaningful connections and you'll stop being preoccupied with your problems. Remember—Give and it shall be given to you. (Luke 6:38).

   When you're generous you are also more likely to develop a sense of gratitude about your current blessings. Thank God for simple things like: good movies, good books, good food and good people. An abnormal pre-occupation with self, increases worry and fear.

   Try this: Every morning (while you're getting ready for work or before you step foot into the office) … focus on listening to the birds sing. This is my favorite simple pleasure in life. I love listening to birds sing. They start their day in song. Before they've even had their first meal, you can hear them giving Glory to God. It's a beautiful thing!

6. **Trust God.** He will meet your needs and do the things you can't do. Having faith/trust will improve your life tremendously. This doesn't mean that you don't have responsibility—but it does mean that you can surrender things that are beyond your control to God for help/guidance.

7. **Develop a spirit of patience.** Attempting to do things that are not on God's agenda for your life results in major stress, anxiety and worry. God reveals His plan for us one step at a time. So relax and surrender to His Love for you. I began the original version of this book three years ago, but I had to learn about developing a niche and the technical aspects of writing a book. I also had to be "processed" spiritually and emotionally in order to be an entrepreneur. Your dream will require a period of preparation.

8. **Develop/increase your sense of humor.** The Bible says that "Laughter [a cheerful heart] does good—like a medicine." (Proverbs 17:22) Indulge in

a hearty belly-laugh at least once per day. It's a simple, natural way to reduce stress. Read the comic pages, go online to find a website devoted to jokes and humor or go see a funny movie.

Top 3 Lipstick Ghetto™ Toxins

I decided to address these issues separately, as they are a daily part of working in the **Lipstick Ghetto™**. These are not easy topics. But they are a reality in the workplace for many women. All three contribute to our stress/anxiety. Here they are:

1. **Jealousy:** Often jealousy is rooted in competitiveness and/or insecurity. If co-workers perceive that you have more talent/intelligence than them you may be the target of their rude behavior. Being promoted or recognized for good work can sometimes alienate you from once friendly office-mates.

    The only viable solution is to "tough it out." Remember that you are in the workplace to do work that's pleasing to your boss and to be adequately compensated for your efforts. Your co-workers' jealous behavior reflects on them—not you. Remember, you don't have to please every person … only the right person!

2. **Gossip:** Gossipers have a need for attention and control. They are always chattering/whispering/nattering about one person or another. It's hard for them to mind their own business.

    Even if their gossip is not intended to harm—the behavior can undermine the level of trust in the office. These busy-bodies create strife and division among workmates. The problem is so insidious that, some companies are instituting 'anti-gossip' office policies.

    For the most part confronting gossip is useless, because you can't force people to like you or be happy for you. If co-workers try to get you to engage in gossip—politely but firmly refuse to participate. In Proverbs 20:19, the Word says: "A gossip can never keep a secret. Stay away from people who talk too much." I've learned that when a person is speaking negatively to me about someone else…. they're probably doing the same to me behind my back.

    The more positive you are, the more people will be interested in getting to know you and help you which may increase your profile and visibility as you navigate your escape from the **Lipstick Ghetto™**.

3. **Backstabbing:** Office backstabbers can be dangerous. They seek to undermine and sabotage your efforts and reputation with deceit—while being cordial/friendly to you in your face. They speak negatively about you to colleagues and/or superiors. Backstabbing can be rooted in jealousy or it can simply be the result of someone not having enough to do (either at work or in their personal life).

The first key to dealing with a backstabber; is to not seek revenge by verbally retaliating against them. You want to approach backstabbers privately in a non-confrontational tone. Be clear and concise in speaking with the backstabber. Simply state that you are aware of what is happening and that you want it to stop (don't use threats). If things don't get better—it may be time to speak with your manager.

BODY

Now that you know how to take care of your mind, it's time to address taking care of your body. Taking care of your body is the beginning of all success! Being sick diminishes your ability to be all you are meant to be. Sickness can also delay your opportunity to leave the **Lipstick Ghetto™**.

The 'No More Excuses!' Health Program:

1. Prepare
2. Exercise
3. Eat Right

Prepare:
Set fitness goals for yourself and stick to them. If you need support or accountability, use the buddy system.

Exercise: Exercise is not only good for the body, but it also increases your self-image and self-confidence. The three keys to a good exercise program are: Endurance, Strength, and Relaxation.

Build Endurance

Get your heart rate up by doing cardiovascular exercises at least 3 times per week. To add fun to your routine, get a pedometer and track how much you move each day. Some cardio-building ideas:

- Biking	- Speed walking	- Jogging
- Dancing	- Playing Tennis	- Swimming
- Rowing/Spinning	- Rollerblading	- Hiking
- Skiing	- Cardio Videos	- Treadmill Jog/Run
- Jump Rope	- Step Aerobics Class	- Water Aerobics

To ensure your ability to handle a new fitness routine, consult your doctor before beginning any exercise program, especially if you smoke cigarettes, have a sedentary lifestyle (i.e. you don't exercise regularly, or don't have any physically active hobbies, have high blood pressure/cholesterol, or have a family history of heart disease.

Start small so that you don't get discouraged. Remember to warm up with walking in place and stretching movements. Cool down with gentle stretches. Check out fitness-based web site, www.workoutz.com, for free online exercise videos.

Build Strength/Flexibility

Strength training tones and slims your body. It also revs up your metabolism, which helps your body burn fat (even while your body is at rest)! Start with 3 to 5 pound hand weights or use a weight machine like those found in gyms. This resistance activity can help build bone density and may even prevent Osteoporosis. If necessary hire a Personal Trainer for 1 or 2 sessions to develop a routine that's tailored to you.

Relaxation

How calm are you most of the time? How tense are your shoulders throughout the day? Daily life can be tense. Starting a conscious relaxation routine can help.

One major contributor to tension is improper breathing. Have you ever noticed how often you unconsciously hold your breath? This pattern of shallow breathing causes excess tension to be stored in your body. The next time you're facing a problem or pondering a situation that's beyond your control, pay attention to your breath. Notice how your body is responding.

Deep breathing is a free and easy way to relax and surrender your concerns to God. Just inhale slowly and deeply, then slowly exhale … releasing all negative energy and tension.

Moving meditations such as yoga and stretching are also helpful in reducing mental stress and physical tension.

Use both deep breathing and moving meditations throughout your day—to create a more present, calmer and happier you.

Don't forget to get adequate sleep and rest. Many women suffer the effects of sleep deprivation, which include loss of coping skills, mood swings, feelings of fatigue and even weight gain. Aim for 8–9 hours of sleep per night. Proverbs 127:2 says, "It is useless for you to work so hard from early morning until late at night, anxiously working for food to eat; for God gives rest to his loved ones." (NLT)

Eat Right

To ensure that you choose the right foods, make more trips to the grocery store. When you stock your home/desk with the right foods, you're less likely to give in to go for the convenience store and fast-food options. (Visit www.mypyramid.gov, where you can get a FREE personalized dietary guide and worksheet!)

1. **Eat Breakfast** Skipping breakfast is a regular occurrence for many women. Health experts agree that, people who skip breakfast consume more calories during the day. Eating a balanced breakfast of a lean protein, complex carbs and healthy fat will kick-start your metabolism … so that you can face your day with energy and vitality. Try scrambled egg-whites (olive oil) with veggies and turkey bacon on a whole wheat slice of bread.

2. **Eliminate or Reduce Refined Carbohydrates (Carbs)**—Your goal is to cut refined/processed flour products, which includes white bread, flour tortillas, crackers and rice cakes. Choose complex carbs, such as brown rice and other whole grains. Avoid white rice, as it is a simple carb and quickly spikes your blood sugar. The fiber in complex carbs helps move toxins from your body … while refined carbs sit in your belly like a brick.

3. **Minimize Sugar** Sweet things can brighten your day. But they can also help you pack on the pounds. This includes sugar from Fruit & Energy drinks and coffee drinks from your favorite barista. These are empty and wasted calories. The next time you're tempted to buy one of these beverages …

look at the nutrition label and see how many hundreds of calories they contain!

4. **Reduce Use of Bad Fats**

    Use olive instead of corn oil, vegetable oil etc. Olive has higher amounts of heart-healthy, mono-unsaturated fat.

5. **Go Green** Adding extra fruits, veggies and beans are a tasty way to pad your meals. Most experts recommend four or five servings each of fruits and veggies, which are high in fiber and health promoting antioxidants. Focus on eating deeply colored produce such as (berries, carrots, spinach, peaches, oranges, green beans, etc.). Try to limit your consumption of high-glycemic "starchy" fruits/veggies (corn, potatoes, etc.)

6. **Watch Portions** Watching how much you eat is important, especially when dining out. Make it a point to not clean your plate. You may even want to start charting the number of calories consumed in a small note book.

7. **Drink more water** Drinking more water will help you to feel full and will also help flush your system to aid in digestion.

SPIRIT

First we covered the Mind, then the Body … now it's time to focus on the most overlooked aspect of your humanity: Your Spirit. When I studied to become a Certified Group Exercise Instructor, I learned about physiology, exercise and nutrition, but nothing about taking care of the Spirit. Regardless of your form of worship or belief, I believe that taking time for God shouldn't be isolated to a particular day of the week. We should make time for prayer/meditation and praise every day.

Your Spirit, also known as Intuition is your direct connection to God. Everyone receives information and guidance from their spirit. Some call it a hunch or a "gut feeling." This communication from God is a powerful tool in designing your life.

Here are 6 Keys Partnering with Your Spirit for Success:

1. **Know the nature of God.** God is Love. God is the source of all creativity. He wants us to be fruitful. His wisdom and insight gives us "knowledge of witty inventions" (Proverbs 8:12). He desires that we prosper in our Spirit, Finances, and Health (this 3 John, verse 2).

2. **Slow down.** Spiritual/Intuitive wisdom comes when you are open and relaxed enough to receive it. You must learn to unplug yourself from the external forces and circumstances of your daily life and create a space for receiving from God. Spend time in the morning to visualize and imagine the life you desire.

   When stressed during the day, learn to pause and re-center yourself with a silent meditation or breathing exercise. This will help you leverage the power of the present ... making you more available to "happy accidents" and other serendipitous events.

3. **Ask.** Prayer is a two-way communication tool. Use prayer as a time when you let your desires known to God. Be clear and specific. Also, use prayer as a time to listen and be reflective on what He has to say to you. Pay attention. You'll often get insights or flashes of wisdom as you practice being still and silent. God reveals things to us through our spirit (1 Corinthians 2:10)

4. **Write it down.** By putting the questions you have in your heart on paper, you open up the possibilities of receiving intuitive information in the form of creative insights and ideas. Writing is also an exercise in reflective contemplation and listening.

5. **Surrender.** Surrender requires trust and detachment from the outcome. Each day practice being receptive to what God wants to do in your life. Prayer and meditation are excellent tools to help develop your openness and attentiveness to the Heart of God.

6. **Obey.** Often your Spirit will communicate with you through excitement or passion. Likewise, if you lose peace or become drained by a certain decision, this is probably a clear message to go the other way. Let peace and enthusiasm be your guide.

   If you make it a habit of ignoring your Spirit's direction, you'll eventually become desensitized to its guidance. So learn to trust what your Spirit says to you. Listen to the words you hear, physical sensations you experience, emotions you feel and words you hear.

   These Spiritual/Intuitive impressions are light posts on your path to success. As spiritual teacher Joyce Meyer says, "You've got to step out to find out." I've also heard it said, "First the gesture, then the Grace."

Words To Live By:

Be still and know ... that I am God
—Psalm 46:10

If I am not good to myself, how can I expect anyone else to be good to me.
Maya Angelou

STEP #3

DARE TO DREAM

What's Covered:
- The $100,000 Question
- Goals Worth Pursuing: What Would You Do If ...

Dare To Dream

> "If your memories are larger than you dreams … you're in trouble"
> —Jesse Duplantis

I want to begin this chapter with an actual conversation I overhead on the bus one day between two women (as we were riding through one of the most exclusive areas in metro Phoenix—Paradise Valley!). The 1st woman said, "This is the one of the most boring stretches of road … the same houses and fences." Then the 2nd woman spoke *her* reality. She said, "I always seem to see something I haven't seen before."

This was classic. I'm so glad I was able to hear this exchange. It illustrates so wonderfully what the lack of imagination and creativity can do. Like the 2nd woman, each day I rode through this area … I was looking for a new mansion to look at. It excited me to think that one day, I could possibly live in an area like that.

Don't ever let your past or current circumstances stop you from dreaming about or visualizing a better future. Even if you ride the bus, shop discount stores, or live in subsidized housing, your future is only limited by what you think is possible.

The $100,000 Question

If you were to receive $100,000 (tax-free) from a long-lost relative, determine how much you would spend on the following:

___ Travel/Vacation	___ Save	___ Invest in Stock Market
___ Pay-off Debt	___ Buy Car	___ Give to Church/Charity
___ Start a Business	___ Give to Family	___ Invest in Real Estate
___ Buy Collectibles	___ Money Market	___ Mutual Fund
___ Annuities	___ Precious Gems	___ Other

Goals Worth Pursuing: Now ask yourself these questions....

1. What would you do if you weren't afraid.

_____

2.   What would you do if you absolutely could not fail?

_____

3.   Where will you be in 10 years if you continue on the path you're on today?

_____

4.   What dreams/desires are you longing to fulfill, but keep putting them off?

_____

Field Assignment:

Create a Dream Collage

To get started, grab a piece of contact paper or small piece of poster board, a pair of scissors, a stack of magazines and some scotch tape. Flip through the magazines and tear out everything that your eye is drawn to, whether it's a word, a phrase, a quote, or an image. Don't stop to study or analyze them, just keep cutting and tearing, putting the clippings in a pile. Once you have enough items to fill your paper or poster board start taping them down.

Hang your Dream Collage on your mirror, so that you see it every day. Once the images are in front of you—study and pay attention to the common thread among the various components. Because you're starting to set your intention for a better life you'll also want to watch for clues and messages in your daily life that relate to your Dream Collage!

REMEMBER: When you reconnect and recommit to your deepest dreams and desires, you will unlock the creativity, wisdom, passion and energy it takes to make them happen!

<u>Words To Live By</u>:

Success is loving life and daring to live it.
Maya Angelou

This is my life. It is my one time to be me. I want to experience every good thing.
Maya Angelou

Help heal society's brokenness by using your artistry. Living on the creative edge means daring everyday to dream of a world beyond the socially constructed barriers that imprison and divide us.

Danny Glover, Actor

STEP #4

DISCOVER WHAT'S IMPORTANT TO YOU

What' Covered:

- Re-assess Your Priorities & Values

Discovering What's Important To You

There's more to Life than just trying to make it through the day. If you're only concerned with checking items off your 'to-do' list, life will pass you buy. It's time to take stock and recognize what you truly value.

By discovering and assessing how you spend your time, energy and money, you have a starting point to re-adjust your life to match what truly matters to you. After determining where you invest your time, energy and money—ask yourself where you need to make changes to more accurately express your true values.

When you think about your life, how do you feel?:

— Trapped	— Bored	— Tired	— Angry
— Bitter	— Frustrated	— Stressed	— Fearful
— Unfulfilled	— Unfruitful	— Drained	— Sad
— Disappointed	— Guilty	— Unchallenged	— Isolated
— Anxious	— Resentful	— Confident	— Delighted/Pleased
— Excited	— Happy	— Energized	— Challenged
— Satisfied	— Fulfilled	— Eager	— Grateful
— Enthusiastic	— Peaceful	— Joyful	— Purposeful

Select 5 items from the list below that describe what you value most:

❑ Family	❑ Personal Organization	❑ Goal Identification
❑ Salary/Income	❑ Freedom/Independence	❑ Creativity/Innovation
❑ Health/Beauty	❑ Fear Reduction	❑ Time Management
❑ Motivation/Inspiration		❑ Decision Making
❑ Life Purpose Clarification		❑ Stress Reduction
❑ Business Start-up/Growth		❑ Authenticity
❑ Relationship Building/Personal		❑ Loyalty
❑ Relationship Building/Professional		❑ Security
❑ Wisdom/Education		❑ Spirituality/God

❑ Friendship   ❑ Prestige   ❑ Power

❑ Integrity   ❑ Leadership/Influence   ❑ Community/Service

❑ Life/Work Balance   ❑ Giving/Generosity

Is your life in line with your values? If not, how can you re-invent and re-adjust your life to match? _____

_____

_____

What restricts you most from living up to your values?

___ Lack of time   ___ Lack of Support   ___ Fear

___ Laziness   ___ Procrastination   ___ Lack of desire/motivation

___ Lack of resources ___ conflicting priorities ___ Other _____

When you think about what matters most to you, what are the three biggest changes you want to make in your life over the next 90 days?

1. _____

2. _____

3. _____

Are you willing to do the necessary work to accomplish these things? If so, when will you start? _____

Can you follow a schedule similar to this one? Yes ❑ No ❑
If not, how can you adjust it to fit your life?

- 8 hours for sleep
- 8 hours for work
- 4 hours for health and recreation (fun, prayer, entertainment)
- 2 hours for doing something for others free of charge
- 2 hours for study, preparation, and planning to achieve your goals

Note: When your values and actions don't match, there's going to be a disconnect. This disconnection will cause you to disengage from life and cause feelings of resentment and misplaced anger.

STEP #5

Take Charge of Your Life: No More 'Ms. Nice Girl'

What's Covered:
- Tap Into Your Personal Power & Learn to Set Boundaries

NO MORE 'Ms. NICE GIRL'

> "My biggest mistakes in life have all stemmed from giving my power to someone else—believing that the love others had to offer was more important than the love I had to give to myself."
> **—Oprah Winfrey**

One of the keys to designing the life you want is being able to tap into your Personal Power. Doing so will help you to establish boundaries of what is acceptable and what is not. If you're suffering from feelings of anger or frustration, it's probably because you've compromised or sacrificed too much of yourself. Use these emotions to help you find a healthy balance between your needs and the needs of others.

Walking in your Personal Power isn't about being a bully or controlling. It's about honoring what you value most. When you operate from your place of power, you stay keenly aware to your wants and needs. Walking in your personal power will also enable you to live your life by design ... and not by default.

Answer these questions to find out if you're giving your Personal Power away:

1. Do you carry a lot of regret, anger or resentment about what has happened to you in the past or about your current life circumstances?

   Yes ❑ No ❑

2. Are you easily hurt, offended, or turned-off by other people's actions or words?

   Yes ❑ No ❑

3. Is it easy for people to annoy, irritate, or anger you?

   Yes ❑ No ❑

4. Do you often feel used, manipulated, ignored or abused/mistreated?

   Yes ❑ No ❑

5. Do you allow others to disrespect, demean, or talk down to you?
   Yes ❑ No ❑

6. To avoid conflict/confrontation, do you give in to what others want—regardless of your true feelings/desires?
   Yes ❑ No ❑

7. Do you trust yourself enough to make "important/big" life decisions on your own? Are you comfortable and confident with your decision making skills?
   Yes ❑ No ❑

8. Do you listen to/act on advice of others against your better judgment?
   Yes ❑ No ❑

9. Is it hard for you to say 'no'?
   Yes ❑ No ❑

If you answered 'yes' to many of these questions, you've got some work to do … because you're probably not very happy with where you life is right now.

The Dynamics of Personal Power:

> Cast not away therefore your CONFIDENCE, which hath
> great recompense of reward.
> —Hebrews 10:35 (KJV)

Your Personal Power or lack thereof comes from 4 major sources: Your Perceptions, Other Women, your Expectations, and your Responses. How would you answer these POWER questions?

1. How do you usually perceive others' actions toward you? (Perceptions)
2. How did women in your childhood cope with life's ups and downs? (Other Women)
3. Do your expectations of others often leave you disappointed? (Expectations)
4. How do you respond to hurt, frustration, anger, betrayal, etc? (Responses)

Here are 5 Ways to Tap Into & Walk In Your Personal Power:

Note: These lessons are valuable for business and life.

- Monitor your self-talk. If you're down on yourself, you're inviting mistreatment.

- Write down the ways that you give your power away. Commit to changing them.

- Set clear boundaries. It's about respecting yourself. See people for who they are not for who you want them to be. Learn to read what's on the lines ... not just what's between them. And respond accordingly.

- Be proactive. Passively waiting for your life to change, won't make it happen.

- Finally, give yourself permission to be "selfish" without feeling guilty. Which is superbly illustrated in a Maya Angelou quote, if you're not good to yourself.... no one else can be good to you either. Schedule time to focus on your wants, needs, desires and goals. Use this "me" time to pray, read about what you want, make plans and take action. Even Jesus had "me" time. He made time early in the morning for himself. Mark 1:35, "... Jesus awoke long before daybreak and went out alone into the wilderness to pray." (NLT)

<u>**Side Note:**</u> Giving away your personal power can lead to co-dependency in both personal and professional relationships. Symptoms of co-dependency include:

- Inability to leave relationships, even when abuse/mistreatment is present. Setting boundaries and using your personal power will enable you to assert yourself.

- Abandonment issues. Feeling that you won't be OK unless the other person is in your life or that you won't be able to find anyone better. Learning your worth and value will catapult your self esteem to new heights.

- More often than not, putting the thoughts, feelings, and needs of others before your own. There needs to be a balance. The Bible tells us to 'Love others, as we love ourselves.' So you must learn to love and respect yourself—before you can love another in a healthy and mature way.

- Feeling that you give more in relationships than you get back.

You can stand up for yourself—without being aggressive (overbearing and nasty). You do this by expressing yourself authentically, with a spirit of compassion. The only way to do this is by:

Asking for what you deserve, want and need—and not accepting less.

Decisions, Decisions

Part of taking charge of your life is making good decisions. Remember question #8 from this chapter's question session? Indecision keeps you stuck and frustrated. Figuring out 'what to do'—when you don't know what to do, can be very intimidating and confusing.

Fear can also cause us to put off making a decision because, we ask ourselves— "What if I make a wrong decision?' But we fail to realize that mistakes can be our best teachers. If we are trusting God—we know that he works all things out for our good—so if you are prayerful when making decisions, you can't go wrong.

Before making a decision, ask yourself these 7 questions:

1. Does this decision support my life's purpose and destiny?
2. What is the best/worst that can happen if I do this?
3. Will this the results of the decision move me forward towards my goals? Or backward?
4. Is the timing right to make this decision?
5. Do I need additional input?
6. What is my primary motive for making this decision? Am I being pressured?
7. Do I plan on committing to this decision once it's made?

10 Steps to Better Decision Making:

1. Define the specific decision to be made.
2. Gather all the information needed to make the decision.
3. List all possible choices and options.
4. Consider all of the possible outcomes for each choice and option.

5. Pray and consider how God leads you to feel about each choice.

6. Relate each choice to your values and priorities.

7. Here is where the rubber meets the road—Pick one possible alternative from your list.

8. Commit yourself to your chosen decision and disregard the others. It's important to concentrate your energies and efforts in one direction.

9. Take the necessary steps to turn your decision into a positive one.

10. Evaluate your progress from time to time—and change your decision and approach as necessary.

Words To Live By:

You don't have to please every person, only the right person.
—Mike Murdock, Wisdom Keys Author

I don't know what the key to success is, but the key to failure is trying to please everybody.
—Bill Cosby

Take me as I am … or have nothing at all.
—Mary J. Blige (From Breakthrough CD)

Not everyone has a right to speak into your life.
—John Maxwell

STEP #6

The Art of Recognition: How to Discover the Relationships, Opportunities & Gifts Already In Your Life

The Art of Recognition (How to 'Live In Possibility')

Each day of your life is filled with numerous blessings. Your ability to recognize these blessings (Relationships, Opportunities and Gifts) will dramatically <u>decrease</u> the time you spend in the Lipstick Ghetto™ while <u>increasing</u> your likelihood of success after you leave. It's vitally important that you allow every chapter in this book to teach you something, because opportunities are often missed because of ignorance or lack of maturity.

Learning the Art of Recognition is about being awake and aware during your daily life. There is value in attending seminars and reading books such as this one, however the knowledge you receive will have a limited effect if it's not put into practice in your everyday life.

To master the Art of Recognition, your goal is to pay attention to the events, people and resources that appear in your life. And to be present in every interaction and situation that occurs throughout your day. How do you do this?

1. **Live Prayerfully**. Make even the most mundane task (i.e. the commute to work, making copies, etc.) an opportunity for contemplation and reflection. This habit fosters your ability to hear from your Source (God), through attention and silence. Prayer is life's greatest time saver.

2. **Pause for the cause**. Everyday, make a real effort to stop and savor the beauty around and within you.

3. **Have an attitude of gratitude**. Being grateful and expressing gratitude opens your life up to even more blessings.

4. **Know that 'It's in there'**. Recognize that you already have everything you need for your success or failure within your own heart. Choose to see the abundant side of life rather than the scarcities.

5. **Live each moment fully**. Commit to accepting both the pleasure and pain of life. Both make you more human and accessible. Use them as 'life teachers', so that you can make the world a better place.

6. **Set It and Forget It**. Set your intention/desire for your life by writing it down in your Dream Journal and/or in your Dream Collage. Then take notice <u>and</u> act upon the pleasant surprises, happy accidents, and special coincidences that occur.

7. **Let Go.** Give up your desire to control "how" and "when" your dreams are manifested. Feelings of anxiety will be your clue that your ego is trying to "make" something happen … instead of letting God/The Spirit manifest your intention or desire. On the path to achieving your dreams, your only responsibilities are to be available and willing!

The Art of Recognition Questions & Field Work:

1. What signs and/or messages have you received from God regarding your dream or destiny?

   _____

   _____

   _____

2. Please list the relationships, opportunities, gifts and resources currently in your life that can help you achieve your dream.

   _____

   _____

   _____

3. For the next week pray and ask God for wisdom and revelation on how to leverage your relationships, opportunities, gifts, and resources to achieve your dream and destiny. Write what happens here:

   _____

   _____

   _____

4. What one thing can you do today to embrace a life of possibility and miracles?

   _____

   _____

   _____

5. What was the last "impossible" problem/circumstance that God helped you with? How did the solution come about?

_____

_____

_____

6. Asking the right question, to the right person at the right time can improve your life exponentially. What one thing do you need to know before moving forward on your dream? Is there a trustworthy person you can "tap" for this missing link? If so, when will you reach out to him/her?

_____

_____

_____

STEP #7

Uncover your Passions

What's Covered:

- Discover your abilities, talents and strengths

Uncover Your Passions

> "Everybody says nothing come' too easy,
> but when you got it 'babe' nothing comes too hard ..."
> —**Prince (Song: Baby I'm A Star)**

I love that song. Sometimes you just have to toot your own horn. And that is what this chapter is about. You are going to take stock of your "Rock Star" abilities. Finding and following your passion will open doors....

The secret to your success will be doing what you do best and what you enjoy. I love this quote by Oprah:

"**Passion** whispers to you through your feelings, beckoning you toward your highest good. Pay attention to what makes you feel energized, connected, stimulated—what gives you your juice. <u>Do what you love</u>, <u>give it back in the form of service</u>, and you will do more than succeed. You will triumph."

Now, keep this quote in mind as you ask yourself these **Six "Passion Finder" Questions:**

1. **What parts of your day excite and energize you?**

For the next seven days, make a list of the daily activities that get you jazzed. Maybe it's training new hires, working out, reading/writing, sewing, helping a friend with a problem, balancing your checkbook, etc. Now sit down and find a common thread among these activities. Study your list and think about how they can be creatively molded into a business concept. Whichever concept resonates the most, begin working on it.

During one of my jobs as an Administrative Assistant, I was responsible for publishing the office's weekly newsletter. I truly enjoyed finding creative workplace tips/tools, researching articles etc. I also enjoyed the positive feedback I got from my co-workers when they received the publication each Monday!

This part of my workday was exciting. It was a clue to several of my passions: Reading, Writing, Helping Others, and Publishing.

YOUR PASSION NOTES:

_____

_____

_____

_____

_____

2.   Who do you admire or secretly envy?

Feelings of admiration and envy often point to subconscious desires. Write down a list of two to three women or men whom you admire/envy. For each name, list the qualities and aspects of their life that fascinate you. Then think about how you can begin to develop these same characteristics. It's not about imitating or copying someone else, this exercise is created to help you recognize your dormant talents and gifts.

I admire entrepreneurial media mavens Oprah Winfrey and Tyra Banks. I'm also fascinated by creative and enterprising men like Thomas Edison and Benjamin Franklin.

YOUR PASSION NOTES:

_____

_____

_____

_____

_____

3.   What do you find yourself daydreaming about?

Daydreams can be your primary gateway to uncovering your passions. Daydreams are visual Spirit Messages that reflect your deepest desires and aspirations. They're the 'day trips' of your imagination. Your daydreams are not limited by your current circumstances or perceived obstacles, nor are they restricted by what you think you <u>should</u> be doing with your life. You may also want to consider what you think about doing first thing in the morning and right before gong to bed at night (when your senses are in abeyance)

Keep a small notebook and pen with you at all times, jot down your daydreams, flashes of inspiration and ideas as soon as you get them. I carry my notebook and several pens with me everywhere I go. So when an idea or thought comes up that would be great for a book or other project, I don't have to rely on memory.

When you get some free time, read through your notebook and pray about what it's trying to tell you. Whatever it is, you'll feel intense motivation and excitement to get to work on it!

YOUR PASSION NOTES:

_____

_____

_____

_____

_____

4. What Do People Complement/Admire You For?

You have something that you do really well (something that you do better than anyone in your sphere of influence)—the kind of thing that makes people say, "You should start a business doing that!" or "Where did you learn to do that!" It is probably something that comes to you so easily that you've never even considered it as a talent or special gift. And that's because your innate ability in a certain area is such a part of who you are that you don't realize that people go to school to learn what just comes naturally to you.

Note: It's also probably something that you'd do for people for free. But the objective of this book is to get you to start making money at what you're passionate about. So if you've been fixing peoples' computers for free, doing peoples' hair for free, or baking people cakes without charging for a profit … STOP. You'll never get rich that way. I'll admit that I use to do the same thing. I know I can be hard, especially with family members to charge for your products/services, but it's the first step in asking "strangers" to pay.

Make a list of the things that people frequently complement you for or ask trusted friends and family members to tell you what they think your natural talents and gifts are.

YOUR PASSION NOTES:

_____

_____

_____

_____

_____

5.   Look around you?

The things you surround yourself with are usually clues to your truest passions. Whether it's books on the deep-sea diving, articles on bird watching or desert recipes, we tend to (subconsciously) collect things that reflect our real desires and aspirations.

Look around your home as a stranger would and notice patterns among things that you collect or use for decoration. There may be indicators of hobbies, passions or pastimes that can lend themselves to a profitable business!

YOUR PASSION NOTES:

_____

_____

_____

_____

_____

6.   What do you do in your free time?

Examine your leisure activities/hobbies. 'What do you do for fun in your spare time?' Or perhaps more appropriately, 'What would you LIKE to do if you had more free time?' Is it possible that people would pay you to teach them how to enjoy it too? What you do for fun can hold valuable clues to unrecognized passions.

YOUR PASSION NOTES:

_____

_____

_____

_____

_____

More Ways to "Insight-ing" Your Passion

Now take some time and look at some of the skills and accomplishments of your career.

Please list the skills and abilities you've gained throughout your career (i.e. Computer Software, Accounting, Marketing, Writing, Publishing, Speaking, Baking/Cooking, Customer Service, Retail, Advertising, Telemarketing, Commissioned Sales, etc.):

_____

_____

_____

_____

Please list all of your accomplishments from high school to present (i.e. Voted Best Dressed, Debate Team, National Sales Rep of the Year, Woman of the Year, Board Member, Olympic Finalist, Marathon Runner, etc.):

_____

_____

_____

_____

**We will return to the exercises in this chapter a little later....

Words to Live by:

As you begin pursuing your passions and long-held desires, a once-inactive part of your soul will 'wake up' and excite you, enabling you to turn your dreams into realities. This newfound inspiration will move you to do great things.

Authenticity sells, so 'Keep It Real." Be YOU and bring your true self to the table ...

STEP #8

Create a Community of Support

What's Covered:
- Dismiss The 'Haters'
- How to Build Your Support Network

Create a Community of Support

Dismiss The 'Haters'

> "When the world hates you, remember it hated me before it hated you."
> —Jesus (John 15:18)

People are like elevators ... they can take you up or bring you down. With this in mind, you need to rid yourself of negative, unsupportive people—people I call 'haters.' Haters consciously or unconsciously try to sabotage your dreams. They are not happy nor are they pleased with your ambition or progress.

When you step out to pursue your dream, haters are bound to show up. Jesus even told us that, "... I send you forth as sheep in the midst of wolves, be ye therefore wise as serpents and harmless as doves." He advised us to be wise in dealing with haters. We are to harmless in our relations with them, without trusting them.

You've probably learned by now, that you cannot trust everyone with your dream. Matthew 7:6 says, "... do not throw your pearls to pigs. If you do, they may trample them under their feet, and then turn and tear you to pieces." So use discernment in sharing your plans with people inside and outside of your inner circle.

Not everyone will support your decision to leave the Lipstick Ghetto™. Whether they are doubters, complainers, manipulators, criticizers, or plain just have a bad attitude—you can stop 'haters' from dragging you down.

Of course, due to certain obligations, it may not be possible to cut all 'haters' out of your life completely, but you can establish some boundaries for your interactions with them. Here's how:

1. **Tune Them Out**. Sometimes you may just have to ignore or simply tune out their negativity.

2. **Reduce Your Exposure**. Choose to limit the time you spend with them. Whether it's at a family gathering or in the workplace, avoid being in conversational proximity to haters. Out of sight, out of mind!

3. **Say something**. There may be times that you have to say something to them to them, like: "I would really like it if we talked about something

more positive." Or simply, "I'm surprised to hear you say that." This leaves the burden on them to defend or amend their last statement.

How to Build Your Support System

The key to creating a community of support is choosing to associate with trustworthy people (in addition to friends and family) who affirm your worth and competence. Two ways of doing this are Networking and Information Interviewing.

To find groups and individuals that interest you ask yourself, 'Who can I serve?', 'Who needs to know what I know?', 'Who knows what I need to know?' or 'Who has done what I want to do?' Joining the membership and/or peer advisory groups are excellent places to start.

Networking:

Networking is an excellent tool for building a support system outside of your friends and family. Fortunately, successful networking doesn't require an extroverted personality. The key to networking is letting the people you meet talk about themselves. We all need each other, so the networking dynamic is about learning how you can help the other person, with the byproduct being getting your need met.

It's not about being manipulative, as people can intuitively sense your motives. So, rather than focusing on what you can get out of the relationship, consider how you can serve the other individual. Then let the law of reciprocity work its magic.

The famous motivator, Zig Ziglar, has said that when you help enough people get what they want, you'll eventually get what you want.

Leverage the power of networking by finding ways to help the other person: Find helpful information/encouragement, Expand their network, Build their business, Save time/Money, etc. *Note: If you plan on being a consultant, be careful not to give away the "store" without receiving payment!)

Another key to effective networking is: Asking questions. Engage the person you meet by asking about what they do, their passions, and challenges. Relationships are built by genuine interest. You can also ask who they know who has been down the road you're traveling, or who they know who's in the business/industry you're interested in.

Give your business card and ask for theirs. Always end the conversation by thanking them and telling them you'll contact them soon. Nurture these relationships with follow up contact such as an email or phone call, mentioning an interesting tidbit you learned about them.

Informational Interviewing: By Wisdom a House is Built

Informational interviewing is one of the most powerful techniques for building your support system. Informational interviews are simply meetings for the expressed purpose of learning about a person, industry, business and building relationships.

It's an effective tactic for identifying resources, prospective clients, customers and/ or partners. Informational interviewing is a dialog that can not only open the door for a future project, but it can also be the beginning of a mentor-protégé relationship.

After identifying the person you want to meet, do your homework. Do some research to learn more about their organization, interests and background. Then write out well-formed questions that will help you identify where you might be of service and how they achieved their success. There are two types of questions you may find useful when informational interviewing.

- Personal Questions: How did you decide on your career path/business? What were some of your challenges and successes that helped you get to where you are?
- Business Questions: What market forces are currently affecting your industry? How do you stay ahead of your competition?

If appropriate extend yourself as a resource for assistance and/or a future meeting.

Leggo' my EGO

Now, a final word on building your support system: If you suffer from the "Super Woman" syndrome, you may have some initial resistance to creating a community of support. Don't let a meltdown or crisis be the catalyst for reaching out.

It's a myth that only men have trouble asking for direction. Women also suffer from the inability to ask for help. Asking for help is a sign of wisdom and maturity.

Whether it's asking your mother-in-law to watch the kids while you go to the library to research your book or asking a friend to help you bake cakes for your new catering business, people don't know you need help unless you ask.

Ask yourself these questions:

1. In what areas of my life do I need the most help right now?

     _____

2. Who in my life is most able to help me in these areas?

     _____

3. When am I going to ask for their help?

     _____

STEP #9

Honor Your Commitment to Yourself

What's Covered:

- A Passage to Think About
- Your Personal Commitment Statement
- Keys to Staying Committed
- The Dance of Destiny: 4 Steps to Getting What You Want

Honor Your Commitment to Yourself

A Passage to Think About …

Until one is committed, there is hesitancy,
The chance to draw back,
Always ineffectiveness.
Concerning all acts of initiative and creation,
There is one elementary truth
The ignorance of which kills countless ideas
And endless plans:
That the moment one definitely commits oneself then providence moves too.
All sorts of things occur to help one that would never otherwise have occurred.
A whole stream of events issues from the decision,
raising in one's favor all manner of unforeseen
incidents and meetings and material assistance,
Which no one could have dreamed would come their way.
Whatever you can do or dream you can,
Begin.
Boldness has genius, power, and magic in it.
Begin it now.

When you decide to 'definitely' commit yourself to the dreams and plans God has given you, expect the unexpected. With that in mind, take a moment to complete your **Personal Commitment Statement** (found on the next page).

MY PERSONAL COMMITMENT STATMENT

For as long as I can remember it has been my dream to _____
_____. In the next 24 hours, I will take the first step to turn my
dream into reality by _____.

I realize that at times, I have been my own worst enemy by _____
_____. I resolve to stop _____ and start ___
_____, in order to
live my best life.

When ever I feel like giving up, I promise to _____
_____. I'm willing to do what is necessary to live
the life I deserve.

_____   _____

    Your Signature   Date

Keys to Staying Committed

> "Proof of passion is in the pursuit!"
> **—Rev. Stanley L. Scott, II**

Here are seven ways to stay motivated and committed to yourself and goals:

- **Pursue** goals that are worth pursuing.
- **Establish** and state exactly what it is you want to accomplish and why. Begin with the end in mind. If you want to become a millionaire so that you can retire to spend your days traveling the world, state that. This picture will help keep you going when the going gets tough. Then …
- **Develop** specific, realistic, actionable and time-targeted plans to reach your goals. Saying that you want to start a business is not enough. You must determine what type of business you want to start, who will be your customers, when you'll open your doors, and how you will do it.
- **Be** consistent in taking focused steps from your action plan. Each day, do at least one thing that brings you closer to achieving your goal.

- **Limit** the number of goals that you work on at any given time. You may want to start a non-profit, but attempting to do it while your starting a new business will probably be too much. Pretend you're a postage stamp and "stick to one thing until you get there."
- **Remove** conflicting and competing priorities/goals. Avoid allowing other peoples' priorities to become your priorities. Even well meaning people have a way of getting you off course.
- **Give** it time to work. Your dream won't materialize overnight. You may have to "toil" in obscurity for a while before you see the 'Promise Land.' Don't despise small beginnings. Your time will come! Galatians 6:9 has gotten me through many times of doubt and unbelief: (So don't get tired of doing what is good. Don't get discouraged and give up, for YOU will reap a harvest of blessing at the appropriate time.)

Honoring your commitment to yourself means you don't betray yourself by saying one thing and doing another. Each time you break a commitment with yourself, you erode your self respect, and eventually you'll lose the ability to trust yourself. So only commit to goals and dreams that you can and are willing to follow. Keep on keeping on!

The Dance of Destiny: 4 Steps to Getting What You Want

To begin, ask yourself this question:

What is the ONE THING that's currently missing from my life and/or work that would make the biggest difference?

_____

_____

_____

Now learn how to HULA your way to successfully achieving that ONE thing.

Harness
Understand
Leverage
Act

These steps are key to getting what you want in life and business:

1. **Harness** the power of your dream using your passion, gifts, and abilities. Doing what you're passionate about will decrease the learning curve and increase your chances for success.

2. **Understand** the cost of action and the cost of inaction as it relates to your dream. There will be a price for progress. Going to the next level will cost you something. The price—You will be uncomfortable (at first). You can choose the discomfort of staying where you are OR you can choose the discomfort of getting to where you want to be.

3. **Leverage** the opportunities, resources and relationships in your life to create an action plan. Utilizing your most accessible and affordable resources enables you to expedite your departure from the Lipstick Ghetto™.

4. **Act** on your plan consistently, not allowing fear, procrastination or challenges to keep you stuck. Physics 101: An object at rest tends to stay at rest. Objects in motion tend to say in motion.

Getting what you want out of life means you must be a goal-aware and goal-oriented woman. **Goals** map out your **destination** and provide the **itinerary** for **your journey to a life that works.**

Bottom Line: Be passionate about doing what's necessary to achieve your dreams! Choose to invest in being committed …

<u>Words to Live By</u>:

> There's no sin in getting weary … the sin is giving up"
> **—Bishop Eddie Long**

> Failures are finger posts on the road to achievement.
> **—C. S. Lewis**

STEP #10

'Do the Hustle!': How to Turn Your Passion into Profit

What's Covered:

- The Power of A Good Idea
- Niche and Grow Rich
- Take Your Passion & Make It Happen Guide
- New Business Checklist
- Plan to Win: Create a Winning Business Plan
- In the Mix: Using the Four P's of Marketing to Your Advantage
- Marketing Success: 52 Ways to Grow Your Business For Next to Nothing

How to Turn Your Passion Into Profit

Five Powerful Elements of a Good Idea ...

Good ideas come from the problems and opportunities around you.
Good ideas require focus and dedication.
Good ideas will help a specific group of people.
Good ideas will generate excitement and buzz.
Good ideas will create generational wealth.

What are some of the good ideas that you've failed to act on? Are you still interested in pursuing any of these ideas?

_____

_____

_____

NICHE AND GROW RICH

So far you've discovered your passions and unique gifts, now let's learn how to turn them into a profitable niche business idea. A niche business offers a product or service that's focused on one "targeted" group of customers within a specific industry.

Starting your company as a niche business will have many benefits. First, it saves you money in advertising. Because you'll be focusing all of your branding and marketing efforts in one area, you won't waste your time chasing uninterested customers. When you niche, you are recognizing that your business can't be everything to everybody.

Secondly, having a niche business allows you to personalize and position your business as a one-of-a-kind offering. Establishing a niche boils down to you setting your product/service apart from others by focusing on your Unique Selling Proposition (USP) or competitive advantage—which you'll work on a little later.

Tips for finding your niche:

1. **Leverage your skills and experience.** Look at your past job and/or personal experience in your chosen industry. Having related experiences will help you determine if the business concept will work. For example, I don't have much child care experience. It would be an uphill battle for me to consider starting a daycare or nursery. I don't have the transferable skills that would translate into success in that industry. Therefore, it would be difficult for me to know what potential customers expect, what they want or what they need.

    If you don't have skills or experience in a particular area, don't despair. If you're truly passionate about a particular industry … do some market research. For example, if you want to become a record producer, but lack experience—visit a recording studio to learn the ropes, interview a record producer, visit local music stores and learn what's hot and what's not, and read industry related magazines/websites, etc.

2   **Leverage your passion.** In the beginning, you're going to eat, sleep and breathe your business, so you better love what you do. Look back at your passions from Step # 7. When you work on something that you're passionate about, your enthusiasm will help you to push through the challenging times of starting a business. Having passion about what you're doing also tends to increase your creativity and problem solving ability. Ask yourself, 'What do I do well enough that people would be willing to pay me for it?' Take a creative look at your resume. Are there hidden passions there?

3   **Look around** Identify voids in the marketplace. Where is there an unmet need in your community? What do you hear people talking/complaining/asking about? Think about a business you can start to meet these needs.

    Find out what potential customers like, what they're willing to pay, and how they want it delivered. Aricka Westbrooks, founder of Jive Turkey, a restaurant featuring fried turkeys saw a need for an alternative to the ubiquitous fast food spots in her neighborhood. She began her business in her Brooklyn, New York backyard! (www.TheJiveTurkey.com)

    As a starting point in your search for a void to fill, look at the groups that you currently belong to and have been a part of in the past (Mothers, Shoppers, Students, Allergy Sufferers, Singles, Artists, Collectors, Christians, Socialites, Writers, Runners, Dancers, etc.) to identify what product/service you can offer. Just be sure that there are enough potential customers in that group to sustain a long-term business.

4. **Know your competition and the marketplace.** Look at the industry you're considering. Who will be your competitors? What are their weak spots? Can you do a better job? Get a phone book or your local Chamber of Commerce Directory (or their website). Identify and research two or three of your competitors. Check out their products/services, prices, quality, press/reputation, etc. Find out what you like and what you don't like about each.

    Based on your research, determine if it's the right niche for you. Can your business be established as a "player" in the given marketplace?

Take Your Passion & Make It Happen Guide

NOW…. using what you already know how to do and what you love, let's design a business that's right for you! The next section will be a guide to turning your passion(s) into a <u>viable</u> business concept. It's not about chasing fantasies, but about pursuing a genuine dream. "[S]he who works her land will have abundant food … but [S]he who chases fantasies will have her fill of poverty" Proverbs28:19 NIV

Think: American Idol, where you see contestants who lack the talent to be a professional singer, yet they chase a dream that's really a fantasy. Yes, they have a passion for music; however they don't have the talent or aptitude for it. Your goal in the following exercise, is to marry **your passion** to the **things you do well** and **what people are willing to pay for.**

How To Turn Your Passion Into Profit

"It's Not Work Unless You'd Rather Be Doing Something Else!"
—Unknown

Below are 25 steps to your matching your passion to a profitable business. You may find it helpful to do this exercise with 2 or three different business concepts until you find the right match for your individual goals.

1.   **What industry would you like to start your business in (more categories on next page)?**

__ Entertainment/TV/Movies

__Government Services

__Technology/Computers/Software

__Manufacturing

__Business Services/Marketing/Accounting

__Wholesale

__Recreation/Leisure/Travel

__Retail

__Construction

__Education/Training/Consulting

__Counseling/Spirituality

__Kids/Day Care/Toys

__Law/Legal Services

__Real Estate (Commercial/Residential)

__Finance/Banking/Insurance

__Home Improvement/Maintenance

__Medicine/Health Care/Pharmacy

__Food/Beverage

__Beauty/Spas/Salons

__Fitness/Weight Loss/Nutrition

__Interior Design/Architecture

__Pets (Products/Services)

__Media/Books/Magazines/Photography

__Event Planning/Weddings/Corporate

__Auto (Sales, Repair, Maintenance)

__Transportation/Courier/Trucking

__Arts/Performance/Music

__Other _____

2. **Using all the Passion Finder questions in Step #7 and Your Dream Collage in Step #3: List the common thread among your hobbies, compliments, daydreams, special talents/skills, and life/work experiences.**

3. Based on questions 1 and 2 above, what type of product or service can you offer that people would be willing to pay you for? After doing market research in the bath and body industry, Jamila White, founder of J. Blossom and Co. (www.jblossom.com), identified a void for natural products for girls.

4. Do you need additional training or certification to gain credibility? If so, how and when will you go about getting this training?

5. How will your product/service meet new and/or existing needs in the marketplace?

6. Will your business be a home-based business? If not, where will your business be located?

7. Do you want to work alone or hire staff? If you want to hire staff, will they be virtual or face-to-face employees?

8. Do you want to be a local, national or global business?

9. Will you be able to outsource any of your daily business tasks?

10. What are your personal financial goals? How much do you need/want to earn?

11. Who will be your major competitors? In a market full of competition, Dawn Fitch, founder of Pooka Inc. (www.pookapureandsimple), continues to differentiate her company. She targets her products to boutiques, hair salons and stores like Whole Foods (where she's in 26 stores). Grab a phone book and identify your primary competitors. You can also do a search in online web directories (www.directory.google.com or www.dir.yahoo.com).

12. What products/services do your competitors offer?

13. How much do your competitors charge?

14. What are your competitors' strengths and weaknesses?

15. What will set your product, service or business apart from your competitors? (How can you make life easier or better for your customers? How can you save them time or money? Etc?) What will your Unique Selling Proposition (USP) be based on— (Quality, Service, Reliability, Price, Convenience, Status/Prestige, Credentials, Customization, Ease of use, etc.)

*Don't be afraid to turn some people off. Remember … you can't be all things to all customers. McDonald's is not trying to be Ruth's Chris Steakhouse. The real estate company "We Buy Ugly Houses" is not trying to be Century 21. Wal-Mart doesn't try to be Nordstrom or Neiman Marcus. You get the point. Each company has carved out its own niche and focuses its energy on doing that one thing well.

Remember, 'Authenticity sells.' Begin thinking about what unique "flair" or personality you can bring to your business.... then capitalize on it.

16. What will be your pricing structure? What did you learn about your competitors' pricing? Pricing can be tricky. If you price too high, you risk turning away your customers. Likewise, if you price too low, you run the risk of appearing to not have real value.

    Of course, be sure to include the cost of providing your product or service—then 'mark up' the price to include your profit.

17. Who will be your target market/customers? (Age, Gender, Marital Status, Education level, Race/Ethnicity, Religious affiliation, Income Level, Where do they live, Shop, What magazines, newspapers, books do they read? What websites to they visit, etc.) This information will be helpful in developing and improving your product or service. It will also help determine how and where to market to your customers. To learn more about developing your target market, Visit www.fedstats.com or www.census.gov to learn more about US demographics.

18. Are there enough customers to make your business a success?

19. Are they eager and able to buy your product or service?

20. How will you market to and attract your customers? How does your competition market to and attract their customers? How can you do it better?

Marketing will be key to your company's success. A little later you'll have a chance to develop a more detailed "Marketing Mix." Here you just want to warm-up your creative "juices" with some quick ideas.

21. What will be your business structure? (Sole Proprietorship, General Partnership, Corporation, or L.L.C.)

Sole Proprietorship: This is the simplest and most common way to start a business. A sole proprietorship is simply a business that is owned by one person. The owner is responsible for all business debts and liabilities. It's a low cost way to begin a company. You can operate it under a name other than your own, by registering a "doing business as" or "dba" with your State or County's Trade Name registration office. You can use your "dba" certification to open business bank accounts.

General Partnership: A general partnership is an association of two or more persons for the purpose of building a business for profit. You can set up your partnership by seeking out an experienced attorney to draw up a formalized partnership agreement. Though partnerships are easy to start, there are disadvantages. The primary disadvantages are: dividing decision-making authority and the difficulty in removing an unwanted partner.

Corporation: A corporation is a business that is set up and formed by law as a separate entity from the person(s) who own it. It (the corporation) has its own rights and restrictions. Forming a corporation limits your personal liability. You must obtain a Federal Tax ID number from the IRS for your corporation, after it is formed. Articles of Incorporation must be published. Corporations can raise funds through offering stock to the public. These shareholders are owners of the corporation. Corporations are usually set up by your state's Corporation Commission.

Limited Liability Company (L.L.C): A Limited Liability Company can have an unlimited number of owners. A LLC offers a business the protection of a corporation. Publication of Notice of Filing of Articles of Organization is required. The LLC structure doesn't require public disclosure of finances. Owners are protected from liabilities of debts of business, although personal guaranty is also likely.

22. Will you need a business loan or will you bootstrap (use your own money)?

23. What will be your business name? Is it easy to spell, pronounce, and remember? Is it already in use by another business? The use of terms, Incorporated, Inc., Corporation, Corp., and LLC can only be used in your business name if you are properly registered with the appropriate government agency. Write down several possibilities for your business:

24. Can you afford to start the type of business that you're thinking about? If not, is there a way that you can adapt the concept so that it's more affordable? You may find that you need to save for 2–4 months in order to get initial start-up capital.

Write down every conceivable cost for your start-up idea (including: opening a bank account, web domain/hosting, business cards, etc.).

25. Reality Check: Take an objective look at your business idea/concept. Determine if there are any limitations or potential problems that you overlooked. Is your business going to be compatible with your desired lifestyle or does it conflict? Does your idea have long term potential or is it simply a fad? Fads aren't necessarily bad … remember the Pet Rock. A fad can fill your bank account too!

Is your business idea feasible? Can it work? Before moving forward on your business, you should probably consider getting a second pair of eyes to help. Get free online and face-to-face business counseling and mentoring from SCORE. For more information, visit: www.score.org.

In addition to free small business counseling, SCORE's web site offers articles, business forms, sample business plans, success stories and more!

Your New Business Checklist

_____ Conduct research on your industry, target market and competition. Then decide exactly what products and/or services you will offer.

_____ Choose a name for your business, research its availability, then register it with the appropriate government agency. Also find a suitable domain name for your business' web site.

_____ Write your business plan.

_____ Determine whether you want to operate as a sole proprietor, partnership, corporation or LLC, etc.

_____ Get a Federal Tax ID number, if necessary. You can get one by phone, online or at any IRS office. Visit www.irs.gov.

_____ Obtain any necessary local licenses and/or permits.

_____ Open business bank account(s). If you're selling anything online, you will want to get a payment processor or merchant account, through your local bank or web sites such as PayPal.com.

_____ Decide how you're going to finance your business (Loans, Investors, Friends/Family, Savings, etc.)

_____ Find the perfect location for your business. Check local zoning ordinances.

_____ Get your promotional materials (Web site, business cards, etc.)

_____ If hiring employees, review applicable labor regulations. Visit www.dol.gov, www.osha.gov, www.sba.gov, and your state's labor department.

_____ If needed, retain a CPA, attorney, insurance agent, etc. You can Also get free financial publications from the IRS, such as: _Starting a Business and Keeping Records_ or _Tax Guide for Small business._

_____ Begin making money. If you need moral support or advice with finally quitting your Lipstick Ghetto™ job, check out this web site: www.i-resign.com.

Plan to Win:
Create a Winning Business Plan

Write the vision, and make it plain upon tables, that he may run that reads it.
—Habakkuk 2:2

What is a Business Plan? A business plan is a "road map" to your business' success. It expresses what your business is, what its structure will be, who will be involved, how it will make money, and how much money it will make—among other things.

Why should you have one? A business plan will help you "flesh-out" your business idea. It will enable you to spot weaknesses in your idea and give you the opportunity to fix them before putting a great deal of time and/or money into it. A business plan is also a tool for getting funds for your business. Lenders, venture capitalists, and angel investors, all look for a well written business plan.

Your business plan will have four basic parts:

1. Executive Summary (i.e. Business Concept)

2. Marketing Plan

3. Management/Operational Plan

4. Financial Plan

1. **The Executive Summary**—Your Executive Summary will be a one page summary of what your business is and its competitive advantage. This is probably the most important section of your plan, because it will give the reader an overall view of your entire business. The Executive Summary should address the following:

   * What industry does your business operate in?

   * What does your business do?

   * What customer needs are being met?

   * What are your sales projections?

   * What makes you unique from the competition?

2. **The Marketing Plan**—Your Marketing Plan will give an overview of several important factors, including:

* **Target market**: Describe potential customers based on age, gender, income, education, occupation, leisure activities, goals, buying habits, and geographic location

* **Competition:** Answer these questions: Who are your major Competitors? What separates you from your competition? Why would potential customers leave your competition to choose your product or service?

* **Market Analysis**: In this section, based on your research, you will communicate your knowledge of your business' industry.

* **Location Analysis:** Indicate your business location and how it will boost or strengthen the sale of your product or service. Also address what the neighboring business are, if there is room for expansion, are renovations needed (if so, how much will it cost), and the status of customer access—i.e. parking, door location, etc.

* **Pricing Structure:** Address how much it costs to acquire or manufacture your product. How does your price compare to your competitors? What image will your pricing project to potential customers? What is the value your customers get for your price?

* **Marketing Strategies:** Describe how you will reach potential customers. Address where and how your customers seek out your product/service. What messages will be communicated to customers and what media is suitable for this communication (advertising). And indicate how you'll evaluate the success of your advertising efforts.

3. **The Management/Operational Plan—**

    a.) **Management Team:** Here you will describe who will run the business, what their business background is, etc. Also indicate who will report to whom. You will also discuss the legal structure of the business (i.e. is it a Corporation, Partnership, LLC, etc.) *in the appendix of your business plan include copies of resumes for key members of management.

    b.) **Employees:** How many employees are needed now and in the future? What skills do they need? How will they be hired and trained? What will be the salary structure? How will personnel polices be communicated to employees?

    c.) **Operations:** Describe how your business will operate on a day-to-day basis and the responsibilities of each team member.

4. **The Financial Plan**—This section is the bread and butter of your business plan. It will detail how profitable your business will be in the short and long term. It also outlines how your business will be funded.

- How much money (capital) is needed to start your business?

- What will be the sources of the needed capital? Can you offer collateral?

- How will the money be spent (i.e. inventory, marketing, acquisitions, etc)?

- How and when will you repay your investors?

- What is the "Plan B" if you cannot repay?

This section also requires supporting financial statements such as the owner's Personal Financial Statement (that lists income, assets and liabilities), a Start-up Costs Statement, an Income Statement (that projects the amount of revenue, cost of goods, expenses, and a Pro Forma Cash Flow Analysis (that details amount of sales, income and expenses—this form should also be done monthly).

In the Mix: Using the Four P's of Marketing to Your Advantage

*People can get many good things by the words they say …
the work of their hands also gives them many benefits.*
—Proverbs 12:14 (NLT)

Marketing is all about the words you use to convey your message to your target market. Your primary tool for doing this will be your Marketing Mix. The four elements of a Marketing Mix are **Product, Price, Placement, and Promotion.** With that in mind, know that your business success will depend four things:

1. Your ability to identify a great market opportunity (Product or Service),

2. Your ability to offer your product at a price that customers are willing to pay and gives you a hefty profit (Price),

3. Your ability to deliver it in a unique and exciting way (Placement),

4. Your ability to get the attention, interest, desire and action of your target market (Promotion)

Your creativity, passion and vision will be vital to creating an awesome Marketing Mix and … ultimately a thriving and profitable business.

Your Marketing Mix will operate as 'command central' for your business. All of your decisions will be based on what's in your marketing mix. The mix is a living document, meaning you will revisit it often to measure your results and to make changes.

Let me warn you. Be careful what you write here … you just may get it. I wrote a "job" version of this mix a couple of years ago. After doing my "market research," I plugged in what was on my heart and set it aside (actually I had totally forgotten that I'd written it).

Two years later, I was going through some paperwork in my closet and I came across it. To my surprise, I had gotten what I'd asked for. I had written that I wanted a job as an Administrative Assistant at a construction company and that I wanted to earn $35,000 per year.

Well, as I write this book I am working at a construction company (we built cell phone towers for wireless companies) and I'm earning a little over $37,000 per year! How's that for results. Although I see my job as a blessing, I wish I had dreamed bigger … (which is why I'm writing this book). Funny how God works things out!

Because of its size, you'll find the" Marketing Mix" exercise on the next page:

YOUR MARKETING MIX ...

Based on the work you've done so far, plug the ingredients into your mix. If necessary, use another sheet of paper.

Product: What are you offering your customers?	Describe:	Indicate your next steps:
*Whether you're offering a product or service be specific about what the customer is getting for their money.		
Placement: How do you plan to get your product to your customers (i.e. distribution method)? *For example: Look at the DVD rental industry. There are three major players. Each of them offering the same product. But each "distributes" them differently. (Blockbuster, Netflix, and RedBox). One sells primarily at stores, one sells only online, and the other sells through fully-automated kiosks at Walgreens.	Describe:	Indicate your next steps
Promotion: How will you get noticed by your target market? How will you differentiate yourself from your competition?	Describe:	Indicate your next steps
Price: How much will you charge for your product or service?	Describe:	Indicate your next steps

52 Ways to Grow Your Business for Next to Nothing

There are numerous ways that you can position your business for greater success. In this section, I will show you 52 <u>powerful and creative</u> strategies to increase the amount of money you earn in your business. Whether you offer products or services—these tips will strengthen and renew the vision you have for your business. Implement one or two of these strategies every 6 months.

Please note: I neither endorse nor recommend any of the companies listed in this book. All resources given are listed as a starting point for your research.

1. Package your products/services so that you receive residual and passive income. How? Automate your business by creating an online tutorial/CD ROM, or audio CD that teaches interested people what you know.

    Learn how to develop online tutorials and training products with software like Adobe Captivate 3 (visit: <u>www.adobe.com/products/captivate</u> or companies like <u>www.delpadre.com</u> or <u>www.CDROMstudio.com</u>).

    If you want to create and sell your own CD products, check out these web sites: <u>www.sfvideo.com</u> <u>www.nationwidedisc.com</u>. (Find companies to ship your CDs for you, such as <u>www.AmazonServices</u>—which offers order fulfillment and drop ship services, <u>www.pickpacklogistics.com</u>, or <u>www.moultonfulfillment.com</u>).

2. Get Certified. Several government agencies and third-party organizations offer certifications that are available to businesses owned by minorities and women. Becoming a Certified Woman—or Minority Business Enterprise (WBE/MBE), can open the doors to doing business with the government and to doing business with Fortune 1000 companies (through their Supplier Diversity Programs). Visit your state's website. Also check out the National Minority Supplier Development Council (<u>www.nmsdc. org</u>), Women's Business Enterprise Council (<u>www.wbenc.org</u>), The Minority Business Development Agency (<u>www.mbda.gov</u>), the CertCities Certification Database (<u>www.certcities.com</u>) and the Small Business Administration (<u>www.sba.gov</u>)

3. Know what product/services that you will not/cannot offer. Avoid spreading yourself too thin. Doing so will also help keep your costs down. Remember, 'grow rich in a niche.' To learn more about running a small business visit: <u>www.smallbusiness.yahoo.com</u>, <u>www.startupjournal.com</u>, <u>www.inc.com</u>, <u>www.entrepreneur.com</u>, <u>www.businessknowhow.com</u>, <u>www.allbusiness.com</u>, and <u>www.sba.gov</u>.

4. Barter to save time and money. Bartering is a simple system of trading what you have to get what you want or need. Remember in school how you traded your sandwich to get what you really wanted …? Bartering can help free up your cash for advertising, inventory, etc. (www.barterbucks. us, www.u-exchange.com, www.tradeaway.com, www.swaptreee.com, www.barteritonlne.com)

5. Each month ask at least 5 customers for referrals. To avoid getting "unqualified" referrals, let your customers know what types of referrals you're looking for. This will decrease the likelihood of you chasing the wrong prospects. Offer your current customers incentives, such as discounts and rebates for referrals who become customers. Remember to immediately acknowledge and follow-up on all referrals.

6. Let your customers know what you can do for them. Your marketing materials should communicate benefits … not features. Customers want to know exactly how you can help them (save time, save money, be happier, more fulfilled, earn more/increase sales, lose weight, etc.)

7. Participate in online forums/chat rooms and discussion boards where you're likely to find your target market. Before participating, be sure that you have something worthwhile to say. Be clear and make every word count.

8. Host a free teleconference/tele-seminar. Use it as an opportunity to give potential customers information on your industry. Avoid making the entire session a "sales pitch" for your product or service. Add value to the attendees. At the end of the session mention your website, book, service, etc. Visit: www.freeteleconference.com, www.freeconference.com, www.instantconferece.com, Or try hosting a web conference: www.gotomeeting.com

9. Use SEO/PPC techniques to drive business to your website. Depending on your industry, both can be relatively affordable ways to increase your business' on and offline sales.

   * Search Engine Optimization (SEO) is the process of improving your web site's content in order to drive more qualified traffic and increase your site's page rank, based on specific key words. It can be as simple as re-writing your site's content, adding a site map, optimizing images with text, etc.

   * Pay-Per-Click (PPC) Advertising is a form of online advertising whereby, business owners bid on search engine key words related to their product or service, in order to get qualified click-through and conversions.

Visit www.seochat.com to learn more about Search Engine Optimization. Visit www.adwords.google.com and www.searchmarketing.yahoo.com to learn more about Pay-Per-Click Advertising. Your local library is also likely to have great books on each topic as well. There are also companies that can help. Visit www.Clicks2Customers.com, www.gatesix.com, www.iclimber.com, www.wordtracker.com and www.sempo.org.

10. Host or be a guest on a local radio or TV talk show. Be sure to choose a program that your target customers listen to/watch. You can even start your own online radio station. Visit: www.Live365.com.

11. Under-promise and Over-deliver to your customers. Going above customer expectations creates loyalty. Susan Brooks, founder of Cookies From Home, embodies the spirit of service. She has a passion for service and it's a part of her business. (www.CookiesFromHome.com and www.ServesYouRight.net).

12. Start a Blog. Blogging is an excellent way to open the lines of communication between you and your customers. This instant communications tool is great for getting free market research. You can learn what your customers want and what they need … simply by asking. (www.blogger.com, www.wordpress.com, and www.typepad.com, all offer free or low cost blogging tools)

13. Conduct focus groups to learn how to improve your company's products or services. Begin your research at one of these sites: www.e-focusgroups.com and www.focusgroupmarketing.com.

14. Don't just offer your business card … ask for permission to call or email all contacts. Then follow through. Learn more about getting business cards and other promotional items at: www.overnightprints.com and www.vistaprints.com.

15. Sell. Sell. Sell. Master the skill of converting prospects into paying clients. Don't be afraid of the word "Sales." Sales is simply believing something and convincing others. To improve your "sales-ability," read sales books, attend seminars, or hire a sales coach. www.amazon.com, www.justsell.com, www.DaleCarnegie.com,

16. Give. When you give, whether it's samples or gifts, to the right people (i.e. influencers)—you open the door to greater opportunities and visibility. Whether it's a book or brownies consider, strategically giving your product to people who can spread the word about your company. Proverbs

18:16: A [woman's] gift makes room for [her] and brings her before great men/women.

Speaking of brownies, for a "Brownie Success" story visit, entrepreneur, Aundrea Lacy's web site: www.luvsbrownies.com.

17. Meet your personal needs outside of your business. Living a life of balance outside of your business is crucial. Check out: www.modernmom.com, www.workingmother.com, or www.parentsinapinch.com.

18. Consider raising your fees … to attract a different type of customer.

19. Deepen your relationship with 10 influential people in your community. Check out: www.MeetUp.com, www.LinkedIn.com, www.NAWBO.biz, and www.facebook.com.

20. Network with other women business owners. To learn more, visit: www.LadiesWhoLaunch.com, www.womanowned.com, www.womenentrepreneur.com, www.modernmom.com, www.enterprisingwomen.com and www.womenpresidentsorg.com.

21. You 'Otta Be In Pictures. Advertise your business on the silver screen. Check out www.screenvision.com, they offer pre-movie spots and lobby advertising opportunities. Another (more costly) possibility is to place your ads on public transit shelters in your community (www.ClearChannel.com)

22. Get "Almost" Free Money. Research ways to get individuals, angel investors or venture capitalists to invest in your business. Venture capitalists usually expect to reap 10–20 times their investment so be sure you've done your homework on your business concept and product. Check out: www.countmein.org, www.Prosper.com, www.goldenseeds.com, www.ventureworthy.com, www.vcapital.com, www.vfinance.com, www.angelcapitalassociation.org, and www.businessfinance.com.

23. Invest 5–10% of your revenues into training and professional development. Use the funds to attend tradeshows, seminars and conferences related to your industry/business. You're sure to learn a great deal and meet great people!

24. Update your business plan. As your industry and target market changes, it will be wise to revisit your original business plan to make improvements on your product/service, promotion, place/distribution, and price. To learn more, visit: www.bplans.com, www.sba.gov/smallbusinessplanner, www.businessplans.org. or www.planyouridea.com.

25. Write a book/ebook that breaks the mold and presents information in a new light. Learn how to write a 'book with a hook' by reading, *Putting Your Passion Into Print*, by Arielle Eckstut and David Henry Sterry (Workman, $14.95) To learn more about self-publishing your book, visit: www.iUniverse.com, www.booksurge.com, and www.xulonpress.com. To learn about traditional publishing visit: www.writersmarket.com To publish an ebook check out: www.Payloadz.com, www.streamingdelivery.com, www.ebookpower.com, or www.digitalgoodsdelivery.com

26. Consider strategic partnerships. Find a complementary business that may help your business position and determine if there are synergies that can be leveraged.

27. Speak to service groups, membership and business organizations at least twice per month. It will increase your visibility as an expert in your field. To learn more, visit: www.speakersnetwork.com, www.professionalspeaker.com, www.toastmasters.org, www.speakingwithoutfear.com, www.speakeasyinc.com or www.publicspeakingskills.com,

28. Send out a monthly newsletter by mail or electronically. Create a publication that gives timely and valuable information in a clear, concise and creative way. Try www.ConstantContact.com or www.iContact.com.

29. Use the phone. The cell phone is such an integral part of most Americans' lives. So, why not use this wireless technology to reach out to your customers.

    Companies like MESSAGEbuzz, offer mobile marketing solutions to businesses around the country ... such as the ability to text customers with information on your business' new products, services, contests, etc. (www.messagebuzz.com) or a company called Enpocket (www.enpocket.com)

30. Anticipate and respond to your customer's needs. In addition, it is important to ask for feedback from customers. Listen and respond accordingly. Get a customer testimonial line. Visit: www.audioacrobat.com.

31. Take a vacation once per quarter. It will re-energize you and help you be more productive. It's true. A vacation can take your business to the next level. Founder of Godaddy.com, Bob Parsons, got ideas for his business while on vacation in Hawaii! Check out, www.virtualtourist.com, www.hostels.com, www.travelchannel.com, www.TripIt.com or www.lonelyplanet.com.

32. Sponsor a fund-raising event for an organization near to your heart. For more information, visit: www.networkforgood.org, www.firstgiving.com,

or www.charitynavigator.org. Strategic generosity always pays. Cast your bread …

33. Write articles on topics related to your business. Then seek to have them published online, in newspapers or in magazines. Websites such as www.iSnare.com, www.eZineArticles.com, www.GoArticles.com, and www.ArticleWritingTips.com may be able to help you get started.

34. Sponsor a scholarship to a local community college or university. Offer a $1000–$1500 scholarship to high school students in your community. Then let the local newspapers and magazines know about it.

35. Host a live conference, seminar or class. Teach a mini-course on a topic of interest to your target market. After the event use evaluation sheets to get feedback and as a source for testimonials to use in your marketing materials.

    Sites like www.EventBrite.com, can help with registration and payment processing for your event.

36. Value your time. Don't waste time on unnecessary tasks. Investigate opportunities to delegate work. Consider outsourcing tasks to a virtual assistant. Check out www.eLance.com, where you can get a virtual web designer, administrative assistant, writer, and more. Or visit www.ivaa.org, www.assistu.com.

37. Alert your college of milestones in your business. Most universities and colleges publish Alumni accomplishments in their Alumni magazine. Getting your information published will give you valuable visibility with other successful people.

38. Join three clubs or organizations where potential clients would likely be members, such as your local Chamber of Commerce or a peer advisory group.

39. Have a self-introduction that is memorable and engaging. Keep to 30 seconds or less. Make it clear, concise and catchy!

40. Learn to buy low and sell high. The woman in Proverbs 31 mastered this skill. She was successful at retailing and real estate, both of which require an eye for bargains.

41. Host home parties. If you offer a fun product, selling it through home parties will enable customers to see and touch it for themselves in a relaxed, low pressure environment. Home parties also give you the opportunity to get live feedback from customers. (www.directsaleshelpers.com)

42. Be Public Relations savvy. Begin your PR campaign by sending out relevant, news-worthy press-releases to reporters of publications that your target market reads (newspapers, magazines, websites, etc.) This is an excellent way to get free publicity for your business. For more information on Public Relations, visit: www.aboutpublicrelations.net., www.prnewswire.com, www.expertclikc.com (where you can list yourself as an expert ... so that journalists can find you) and www.pr.com.

43. Get online. If you don't have a website ... it is vital that you get one. More and more business is conducted online. Check out: www.1and1.com, www.GoDaddy.com, www.Register.com,

44. Set specific goals for your business. Write these goals down, then identify specific activities that need to be done to accomplish them. Then each day do one or more things that will get you there. Check out www.mygoals.com. For a small monthly fee, the site helps you to set, manage and achieve personal and business goals.

45. Don't wait or procrastinate. Take the initiative and get started on ideas and projects that you have been sitting on. If you need help remembering things sign up for a free email reminder service (www.iwantsandy.com, www.memotome.com, or www.onlininereminders.net). Be sure to research them thoroughly before giving your email address. You don't want an inbox full of spam.

46. Tie your service or product into a 12 month calendar based on seasons and holidays. (i.e. January: New Year's Day/Martin Luther King Day, etc.). You can also gain publicity for your business by tying it to current trends or events (i.e. a best-selling movie/book, popular TV show, current fashion trend, etc.)

    Tamicia Currie got great publicity in a local newspaper for her new children's book, *Peanut Butter & Sweet Potato Pie*, by tying it to Black History month (www.thejuiceandberries.com).

47. Get Celebrity Endorsements. The right celebrity endorsement can catapult your business' credibility and "street-cred." Check out these web sites: www.CelebrityBrokers.com, www.CelebrityEndorsements.com, or www.ContactAnyCelebrity.com. Remember local celebrities (news anchors, athletes, business owners) count, too!

48. Participate in an online affiliate program. Affiliate programs allow other website owners to sell your products and services for a commission on the sale. Visit www.Clickbank.com, www.AffiliateGuide.com, www.CJ.com,

www.Linkshare.com. If appropriate for your site, you can also earn extra money from your website by using one or more of these services.

49. Consider working from a virtual office. Virtual office space companies offer you a prestigious mailing address, phone answering services, internet access, meeting rooms, and more at a fraction of the cost of signing a long term commercial lease. (Examples: www.Regus.com or www.YourCityOffice.com)

50. Tithe. Give and you shall receive. It's true. I had been looking for a blockbuster idea, to get my business off the ground. I'd been tithing and praying. Finally, in prayer, I reminded God of what He promised in Malachi Chapter 3. Where he said that if I tithed, He would send great blessings. The very next day, He gave me the title and concept for this book! Note: Tithing also keeps you from doing the right thing at the wrong time (your vine will not cast its fruit before its time).

51. Find a mentor. Building a relationship with someone who is a few steps further down the road to success can make a big difference. A good mentor will challenge you to bring your "A" game to everything you do. (For info on finding a mentor www.mommymentors.com, www.LadiesWhoLaunch.com, or to become a mentor check out The ATHENA Global Links® Program, www.athenafoundation.com)

52. K.I.S.S. "Keep It Simple Sweetie" Avoid creating products or services that are too complicated. You should be able to sum up what your business does in one sentence. Even if your product/service is new, revolutionary and different … it should still be simple and uncomplicated. Confused customers don't buy!

Consider the business idea that God gave the widow in 2 Kings 4, He told her to sell the oil she had in her home. His instructions and the concept was simple. A modern day version of this is story is Lisa Price, founder of Carol's Daughter, a line of exclusive bath and body products. She started her company from her kitchen with less than $200.00.! (www.CarolsDaughter.com)

Here are some other helpful resources.

A few books that I've listened to and read:

- Rich Dad, Poor Dad (by Robert Kiyosaki) *Audio Book
- Who Moved My Cheese? (by Spencer Johnson, MD) *Audio Book
- The E-myth Revisited (by Michael Gerber) *Audio Book
- Think And Grow Rich (by Napoleon Hill)
- The Power of Positive Thinking (by Norman Vincent Peale)
- How To Hear From God (by Joyce Meyer)
- Multiple Streams of Income (by Robert G. Allen)
- Selling Among Wolves: Without Joining The Pack (by Michael Q. Pink)
- The Medici Effect : Breakthrough Insights at the ... (by Frans Johansson)
- Juice: The Creative Fuel That Drives World Class ... (by Evan Schwartz)
- Do What You Are (by Paul D. Tieger and Barbara Barron
- Bootstrapper's Success Secrets (by Kimberly Stansell)
- Success Never Smelled So Sweet (by Lisa Price and Hilary Beard)
- Starting From Scratch (by Wes Moss)
- The Prayer of Jabez (by Bruce Wilkinson)
- Zero Debt (by Lynnette Khalfani)
- Putting Your Passion Into Print (by Arielle Eckstut and David Sterry)
- The Dream Giver (by Bruce Wilkinson)
- The 4-Hour Workweek (by Timothy Ferriss)

A few magazines that I read regularly:

- Entrepreneur
- Essence
- Oprah
- Black Enterprise
- Pink
- Fast Company

Home-Based Business Ideas ...

- Book Sales (New & Used)
- Computer Repair
- Mail-Order
- Web Design
- Newsletter Publishing
- Community/Neighborhood Newspaper
- Cooking Classes
- Hair Stylist/Manicurist
- Seamstress/Tailoring
- Laundry Service
- Lunch/Dinner Preparation (Catering)
- Employee Training/Development
- Resume Writing
- Career Coaching
- Business Coaching
- Virtual Administrative Support
- Researcher
- Instructional Design
- Arts, Crafts, Jewelry
- Information Products (eBooks, CD-ROMS, etc.)
- Day Care/Nanny
- Marketing or Management Consultant
- House Cleaning
- Dog Walking/Grooming/Daycare
- Graphic Design
- Home Parties
- Senior Care Services
- College Planning Consultant

- Personal Concierge
- Inventor
- Image Consultant
- Carpet Cleaning
- Writer
- Head-Hunter
- Real Estate Investor
- Online Retailer
- Employee Assistance Counselor
- Seminar Speaker
- Proofreader/Editor/Typist
- Photographer
- Concert Promoter
- Personal Trainer
- Apparel/Accessories Designer
- Music Lessons
- Tutor (Reading, Math, Science etc.)

More Words To Live By ...

Inspirational Quotes on SUCCESS, COURAGE & CREATIVITY ...

Success

You've achieved success in your field when you don't know whether what you're doing is work or play.
Warren Beatty (1937–)

For you to be successful, sacrifices must be made. It's better that they are made by others, but failing that; you'll have to make them yourself.
Rita Mae Brown

Eighty percent of success is showing up.
Woody Allen (1935–)

The truth is that all of us attain the greatest success and happiness possible in this life whenever we use our native capacities to their greatest extent.
Dr. Smiley Blanton

What's money? A man is a success if he gets up in the morning and goes to bed at night and in between does what he wants to do.
Bob Dylan (1941–)

Courage

Courage is saying, "Maybe what I'm doing isn't working; maybe I should try something else."
Anna Lappe, *O Magazine, June 2003*

The bravest thing you can do when you are not brave is to profess courage and act accordingly.
Corra Harris

The courage to be—is the courage to accept oneself, in spite of being unacceptable.
Paul Tillich (1886–1965)

The highest courage is to dare to appear to be what one is.
John Lancaster Spalding

You can't try to do things. You simply must do things.
Ray Bradbury (1920–)

Creativity

A hunch is creativity trying to tell you something.
Unknown

Creativity is allowing yourself to make mistakes. Art is knowing which ones to keep.
Scott Adams (1957–), 'The Dilbert Principle'

When we are angry or depressed in our creativity, we have misplaced our power. We have allowed someone else to determine our worth, and then we are angry at being undervalued.
Julia Cameron, The Vein of Gold

Live out of your imagination, not your history.
Stephen Covey, The 7 Habits of Highly Effective People

W. Clement Stone Quotes: (Founder of a company I worked for)

- If there is something to gain and nothing to lose by asking, by all means ask!

- If you employed study, thinking, and planning time daily, you could develop and use the power that can change the course of your destiny.

- Sales are contingent upon the attitude of the salesman—not the attitude of the prospect.

- Stand up. Raise your arms. Repeat after me: I feel healthy! I feel happy! I feel terrific!

- To every disadvantage there is a corresponding advantage.

- When our attitude towards ourselves is big, and our attitude toward other is generous and merciful, we attract big and generous portions of success.

- When you discover your mission, you will feel its demand. It will fill you with enthusiasm and a burning desire to get to work on it.

978-0-595-50772-6
0-595-50772-7

www.ingramcontent.com/pod-product-compliance
Lightning Source LLC
Chambersburg PA
CBHW021949200526
45163CB00018B/1347